Workplace Violence
Issues in Threat Management

Workplace Violence: Issues in Threat Management defines what workplace violence is, delves into the myths and realities surrounding the topic, and provides readers with the latest statistics, thinking, and strategies in the prevention of workplace violence. The authors, who themselves have implemented successful workplace violence protection programs, guide novice and experienced practitioners alike in the development of their own programs.

Christina M. Holbrook co-leads The Boeing Company's Enterprise threat management program. Over the past 30 years with Boeing, Christina has worked on a variety of security assignments, which include leading the development and deployment of the company's threat management (workplace violence) program in 1999, as well as serving as a regional and Enterprise specialist. Christina has been an active member of the Association of Threat Assessment Professionals (ATAP) since 1997 (national and Seattle chapter).

David E. Bixler co-leads The Boeing Company's Enterprise threat management program. Mr. Bixler was a corporate investigator with Boeing prior to his current assignment. He has been involved with the company's threat management program for the last 20 years as a site threat management team (TMT) leader, regional and enterprise focal. For the past 25 years, he has been a reserve police officer with the Newport Beach Police Department working in patrol and is a member of the Special Weapons and Tactics (SWAT) team. David has been an active member of the Association of Threat Assessment Professionals (ATAP) since the late 1990s (national and Los Angeles chapter).

Eugene A. Rugala is principal of Eugene A. Rugala and Associates LLC, a behavioral science, consultation, training, and research firm located in Beaufort, South Carolina. He was formerly of the Federal Bureau of Investigation's (FBI) Critical Incident Response Group (CIRG). He was assigned to the National Center for the Analysis of Violent Crime (NCAVC), FBI Academy, Quantico, Virginia. Supervisory Special Agent Rugala was assigned to the NCAVC from February 1995 until his retirement in September 2005. Prior to retiring from the FBI, Mr. Rugala was unit chief of Behavioral Analysis Unit – 1, Threat Assessment and Counter Terrorism.

Carri Casteel, MPH, PhD, is an associate professor of Occupational and Environmental Health at the University of Iowa (UI). She is also the associate director for the UI Injury Prevention Research Center and director for the Occupational Injury Prevention Program of the Heartland Center for Occupational Health and Safety. Dr. Casteel's primary areas of research include workplace violence prevention in the retail and healthcare industries, methods for reaching small businesses with occupational safety and health programs, older adult falls prevention, and prevention of prescription opioid abuse and overdose. She is the past president of the national professional association, the Society for the Advancement of Violence and Injury Research.

Workplace Violence

Issues in Threat Management

Christina M. Holbrook, David E. Bixler, Eugene A. Rugala and Carri Casteel

Routledge
Taylor & Francis Group

LONDON AND NEW YORK

First published 2019 by Routledge

2 Park Square, Milton Park, Abingdon, Oxfordshire OX14 4RN
52 Vanderbilt Avenue, New York, NY 10017

Routledge is an imprint of the Taylor & Francis Group, an informa business

First issued in paperback 2019

Library of Congress Cataloging-in-Publication Data
Names: Holbrook, Christina M., author. | Bixler, David E., author. | Rugala, Eugene A., author.
Title: Workplace violence : issues in threat management / Christina M. Holbrook,
David E. Bixler, Eugene A. Rugala and Carri Casteel.
Description: First Edition. | New York : Routledge, 2018. | Includes bibliographical references and index.
Identifiers: LCCN 2018000565 | ISBN 9781498735124 (hardback) | ISBN 9781315369686 (ebook)
Subjects: LCSH: Violence in the workplace. | Violence in the workplace–Prevention.
Classification: LCC HF5549.5.E43 H635 2018 | DDC 658.4/73–dc23
LC record available at https://lccn.loc.gov/2018000565

ISBN: 978-1-498-73512-4 (hbk)
ISBN: 978-0-367-47134-7(pbk)

Typeset in Bembo
by Out of House Publishing

Contents

Authors

David E. Bixler co-leads The Boeing Company's Enterprise threat management program. Mr. Bixler was a corporate investigator with Boeing prior to his current assignment. He has been involved with the company's threat management program since 1996 as a site threat management team (TMT) leader, regional and Enterprise focal. He has been a reserve police officer with the Newport Beach Police Department since 1992 working in patrol and is a member of the SWAT team. Dave has been an active member of the Association of Threat Assessment Professionals (ATAP) since the late 1990s (national and Los Angeles chapter).

David has participated in the Worker-on-Worker Violence: Development of Methods to Evaluate Policies and Procedures study "Workplace Violence Investigations and Activation of the Threat Management Teams in a Multinational Corporation," published in *Journal of Occupational and Environment Medicine* (November 2013).
He has also co-authored:

- *Security Journal* "The Threat Management Assessment and Response Model: A Conceptual Plan for Threat Management and Training" (July 2015)
- *Workplace Violence Prevention Survey: Findings from ATAP Corporations* (December 2014)
- *Workplace Violence Prevention Survey: Findings from Mid-Sized Companies* (December 2015)
- *Workplace Violence Prevention Survey: Findings on Domestic Violence Programs* (December 2015)

Carri Casteel, MPH, PhD is an associate professor of Occupational and Environmental Health at the University of Iowa (UI). She is also the associate director for the UI Injury Prevention Research Center and director for the Occupational Injury Prevention Program of the Heartland Center for Occupational Health and Safety. Dr. Casteel's primary areas of research include workplace violence prevention in the retail and healthcare industries, methods for reaching small businesses with occupational safety and health programs, older adult falls prevention, and prevention of prescription opioid abuse and overdose. She is the past president for the national professional association, the Society for the Advancement of Violence and Injury Research.

Michael A. Crane is an Illinois licensed attorney and private detective. He is General Counsel for The Lake Forest Group in Lake Forest, IL and specializes in conducting security and behavioral threat assessments, and workplace investigations where allegations have been made by an employee against the company alleging harassment, discrimination, criminal activity, threats of violence, and so on. He also conducts training in workplace violence prevention and active shooter response.

Mr. Crane has been designated a certified protection professional (CPP) by ASIS International (ASIS) and is a certified fraud examiner (CFE). He was a founding member of the ASIS Standards and Guidelines Commission, oversaw the development of the first Workplace Violence Prevention American National Standards Institute (ANSI) Standard, and is currently overseeing a new Active Assailant Standard. He is also the program director for the ASIS Asset Protection II Course. He is a member of the Chicago Chapter of the Association of Threat Assessment Professionals (ATAP) and formerly served as a member of their National Board of Directors. He is a member of the Illinois and Chicago Bar Associations, the Association of Corporate Counsel, and the North Shore Labor Counsel.

Mr. Crane is a 2009 graduate of the Executive Leadership Program of the Department of Homeland Security's Center for Homeland Defense and Security at the Naval Postgraduate School in Monterey, California.

Matthew W. Doherty is the senior vice president leading the Threat + Violence Risk Management practice at Hillard Heintze and the retired US Secret Service Special Agent in Charge of the National Threat Assessment Center. Doherty is a nationally recognized workplace violence prevention and program development expert. Assessing the potential for danger and preventing targeted violence against our nation's leaders and US corporations has been the cornerstone of his career.

Credited with saving lives by intervening in domestic abuse, terminations, severe mental illness, and other critical situations in today's workforce, Matthew advises federal agencies and private-sector organizations by gathering and assessing information about persons or groups who may have the interest, motive, intention, and capability for violence. He has conducted training on threat assessment and targeted violence prevention for law enforcement personnel, schools, and Fortune 500 companies. Featured in numerous magazines, newspapers, and news media for his insights on insider threats, assassinations, and school shootings, Matthew is a sought-after speaker and interview subject on targeted violence incidents and prevention efforts.

Christina M. Holbrook co-leads The Boeing Company's Enterprise threat management program. Over the past 30 years with Boeing, Christina has worked on a variety of security assignments, which include leading the development and deployment of the company's threat management (workplace violence) in 1996, as well as serving as a regional and Enterprise specialist. Christina has been an active member of the Association of Threat Assessment Professionals (ATAP) since 1997 (national and Seattle chapter). In August 2017, Christina received the ATAP Meritorious Service Award.

Christina has participated in the research projects Behavioral Science Guidelines for Assessing Insider Threats (July 2008) and Worker-on-Worker Violence: Development of Methods to Evaluate Policies and Procedures study "Workplace Violence Investigations and Activation of the Threat Management Teams in a Multinational Corporation," published in *Journal of Occupational and Environment Medicine* (November 2013).
She has also co-authored:

- *Security Journal* "The Threat Management Assessment and Response Model: A Conceptual Plan for Threat Management and Training" (July 2015)
- *Workplace Violence Prevention Survey: Findings from ATAP Corporations* (December 2014)
- *Workplace Violence Prevention Survey: Findings from Mid-Sized Companies* (December 2015)
- *Workplace Violence Prevention Survey: Findings on Domestic Violence Programs* (December 2015)

Pamela A. Paziotopoulos began her career as a prosecutor for the Cook County State's Attorney's office in 1990 and quickly focused on the area of domestic violence. In 1996, she joined the American Prosecutor's Research Institute's Criminal Prosecution Division as a Senior Attorney traveling to 38 of the 50 states, conducting training and speaking on domestic violence. In 1997, she was recruited to the Cook County State's Attorney's Office to create and supervise the Domestic Violence Division. She monitored the prosecution of more than 100,000 domestic violence cases emanating each year from the city of Chicago and surrounding area. She served as chairperson and member of various domestic violence committees throughout Cook County and the state of Illinois. In 2002, Ms. Paziotopoulos left the Cook County State's Attorney's office to form her own consulting group, serving both the public and the private sector.

Ms. Paziotopoulos has developed and presented numerous training sessions on the topic of domestic violence and stalking to corporations, prosecutors, advocates, judges, law enforcement agencies, psychologists, shelter personnel, and court watchers. She has trained the Albanian National Police on domestic violence policy and procedures in Tirana, Albania. Ms. Paziotopoulos has frequently been a keynote speaker on domestic violence at conferences throughout the United States. She has also appeared on CNN, CNBC, and the Oprah Winfrey Show, as well as numerous national radio and news stations. She has authored numerous articles on the issues of domestic violence and stalking. Her article "Violence Against Women Act: Federal Relief for State Prosecutors" has been cited by Federal Courts of Appeal as decisive in defending the landmark legislation Violence Against Women Act. In July 2000, she was selected by *Today's Chicago Woman* as one of 100 women making a difference in Chicago. She is licensed to practice law in Illinois and in Federal Court.

Corinne Peek-Asa is the Associate Dean for Research of the University of Iowa, College of Public Health and Professor of Occupational and Environmental Health. She is the director of the CDC-funded Injury Prevention Research Center and also directs a National Institutes of Health (NIH)-funded International Trauma and Violence Research Training program. Dr. Peek-Asa is an injury epidemiologist, and her work focuses on the implementation and evaluation of programs and policies to prevent acute traumatic injuries and violence. She is an appointed committee member of the Transportation Research Board, and she helped establish and served as the president of the Society for the Advancement of Violence and Injury Research. She was named a ResearchAmerica! Public Health Hero in 2010.

Marizen Ramirez is an associate professor at the University of Minnesota, Division of Environmental Health Sciences. She is an epidemiologist by training with experience in mixed methods and intervention evaluation. She has evaluated a number of public health prevention and intervention strategies: policies to prevent and respond to face-to-face and cyberbullying; school- and hospital-based programs of psychological first aid and trauma-informed care to reduce the impacts of trauma; household disaster preparedness programs; and policies and parent-based programs to prevent roadway traffic crashes involving agricultural workers and youth. She has led grants from NIH, CDC, the Patient-Centered Outcomes Research Institute (PCORI), and the National Institute of Justice (NIJ).

Eugene A. Rugala, principal of Eugene A. Rugala and Associates LLC, a behavioral science, consultation, training and research firm located in Beaufort, South Carolina, is formerly of the Federal Bureau of Investigation's (FBI) Critical Incident Response Group (CIRG). Mr. Rugala was assigned to the National Center for the Analysis of Violent Crime (NCAVC), FBI Academy, Quantico, Virginia. Supervisory Special Agent Rugala was assigned to the NCAVC from February 1995 until his retirement in September 2005. Prior to retiring from the FBI, Mr. Rugala was unit chief of Behavioral Analysis Unit – 1, Threat Assessment and Counter Terrorism.

Mr. Rugala, one of the FBI's "profilers" in the unit made famous by the book and movie *The Silence of the Lambs* and the television show "Criminal Minds," specializes in the detailed behavioral analysis of violent crime, including homicide, sexual assault, intimate partner violence, and stalking. These analyses are provided to requesting law enforcement agencies in the form of offender profiles, crime scene analysis, investigative and interview strategies, media and crisis communication strategies, and threat assessments. Mr. Rugala also consults with many corporations and universities in developing and implementing procedures and protocols for the prevention of violence in the workplace and in schools, including threat assessment and management services.

Mr. Rugala has participated in ongoing research regarding stalking behavior, serial rape, and intimate partner, workplace, and school violence. Mr. Rugala has contributed to a number of publications dealing with workplace violence, school violence, and stalking behaviors. Mr. Rugala was involved in research with the University of Iowa and University of North Carolina Injury Prevention Centers under a NIOSH-funded grant to evaluate workplace violence prevention programs in companies throughout the United States. Mr. Rugala is a member of ASIS International, has been a featured speaker on workplace violence prevention and threat management at their national conference in the past, and has assisted in the writing of the ASIS/Society for Human Resource Management (SHRM) American National Standard entitled *Workplace Violence Prevention and Intervention*. Mr. Rugala is also a national advisory board member of the Corporate Alliance to End Partner Violence, a group of Fortune 500 companies who have come together to raise awareness and suggest strategies for companies to deal with intimate partner violence and its impact on the workplace. Mr. Rugala is past president of the Washington, DC chapter of the Association of Threat Assessment Professionals (ATAP). Mr. Rugala has contributed to the content and participated in the video production of *Shots Fired: Guidance for Surviving an Active Shooter Situation, Flashpoint: Recognizing and Preventing Violence in the Workplace*, and *Silent Storm: Intimate Partner Violence and Stalking and Its Impact on the Workplace*. Versions of these programs have been developed for university settings as well.

Mr. Rugala has testified before the Committee on Education and the Workforce, U.S. House of Representatives, regarding workplace violence as a problem in America's workplaces; has testified before the judiciary committees of the Maryland State House and Senate regarding stalking behaviors on behalf of the Maryland Family Violence Council sponsoring revised stalking legislation; has testified before the South Carolina House Committee on Domestic Violence Reform; is a past board member of the South Carolina Coalition against Domestic Violence and Sexual Assault in Columbia, South Carolina; has provided expert testimony in several trials dealing with assessing dangerousness in stalking and intimate partner violence; and has been a guest lecturer at numerous corporate conferences on workplace violence and at police schools throughout the United States, including the FBI National Academy, as well as police schools in England, France, Germany, Australia, Japan, and the former Soviet Union.

Mr. Rugala has consulted with the Protection Detail of the British Royal Family regarding Public Figure and Celebrity Stalkers. Mr. Rugala has also consulted with members of New Scotland Yard regarding mass murder, specifically as it applies to workplace and school violence. Mr. Rugala has been interviewed by various media organizations regarding intimate partner violence, stalking, workplace and school violence, and sexual assault, as well as other violent crime issues.

Mr. Rugala holds a Bachelor's degree in Biology from Penn State University and has taken graduate courses in Public Administration at the University of New Mexico.

Mr. Rugala was employed with the FBI for 31 years and was previously assigned to FBI offices in Santa Fe, New Mexico, Fayetteville, North Carolina, Washington, DC and Quantico, VA.

Foreword

By Andre Simons

"BREAKING NEWS: there are unconfirmed reports of an active shooting with multiple casualties …"

These words are ones that no person ever wants to hear. This headline typically means that someone has decided that destructive violence is the only solution to his or her problem. These words reflect the terrible moments when days, weeks, or even months of planning culminate in a sickeningly familiar script as an offender wreaks unimaginable havoc upon the employees of a company, the students in a school, or neighbors living and working in a community. After repeatedly hearing these horrible broadcasts over the news each year—and with evidence that such attacks are on the rise—it may be tempting to yield to the notion that little can be done to prevent targeted violence in the workplace.

The statistics are sobering to say the least. According to the FBI's Active Shooter study released in September 2014, the years 2007–2013 experienced an average of 16.4 active shooting incidents each year. Of the 160 active shooting events that occurred between 2000 and 2013, the largest percentage (45.6%, $n=73$) impacted areas of commerce. While an active shooting remains one of the worst case scenarios for any business or corporation, there are also a myriad other concerns that can impact workplace safety: insider threats from disgruntled employees who perpetrate kinetic or non-kinetic hostile acts; external threats against safety from consumers or indirect affiliates; completely unaffiliated outsiders targeting employees and customers for victimization; ideologically opposed or radicalized individuals who attack a corporation based on philosophical differences or symbolic significance; and profit-driven crimes. It is not unrealistic to suggest that as you read this, someone is contemplating and/or actively planning to commit an act of violence against a place of business or commerce. For safety and security stakeholders charged with protecting their organizations from internal and external threats, these concerns are not just theoretical concepts on the page—they exist as a mission priority that must be met and conquered every day. A tough job, to be sure, one that comes with immense pressure to be accurate and effective—not just sometimes, but all the time.

As described by Aristotle, "Pleasure in the job puts perfection in the work." Yet, employees living under the constant specter of workplace violence can hardly be expected to find either pleasure or perfection amidst overwhelming anxiety and fear. Whether recovering from a catastrophic attack or struggling day-to-day with an aggressive office bully, the physical, psychological, and emotional costs of violence that impact employees cannot be overstated. If a workforce lacks confidence in management's ability or will to implement effective prevention and response measures, morale suffers and productivity wanes. Violence, the threat of future violence, and the recovery from past violence all contribute to a corrosive, enterprise-wide toxicity.

Less important, but still critical to the success of any company, is the economic impact of workplace violence. As described by the U.S. Department of Labor, the adverse impact of violence on organizations and individuals is wide-ranging and can include: the temporary/

permanent absence of skilled employees; impediments to productivity; the diversion of management resources; and increased workers' compensation costs. Responsible, ethical, and sound management means not only preparing for crisis management and response to an attack but implementing prevention efforts to disrupt and detect a problem before the victimization of employees occurs.

Such prevention efforts have been complicated in recent years by a perceptible shift in the "threatscape," the spectrum wherein a potentially violent offender collides with and deliberately manifests hostile acts against an individual, institution, facility, or public space. The trends and patterns of today's threatscape reflect the complex issues involved in mitigating workplace violence and necessitate an agile response from dedicated threat assessment and management professionals. The three most daunting challenges in the new threatscape include:

1) The role of social media and the copycat phenomenon. The ubiquitous, relational, and instantaneous nature of social media can often match an offender's desire for externally validated infamy and notoriety. Recent workplace violence attacks such as the shooting of a Roanoke, Virginia, television news reporter and her cameraman tragically demonstrate how an offender can use social media platforms to broadcast his or her carnage concurrently with the offense. With the knowledge that active shooters often study and/or mimic past attackers, security and safety professionals need to recognize how social media can potentially be used to announce an imminent attack while understanding the role such "broadcasts" may play in inspiring future perpetrators of violence.

2) Inter- and intra-organizational communication and information-sharing. A holistic approach to assessing and managing a person of concern often demands a "cross-pollination" of information within an organization and between companies or agencies. An employee who demonstrates problematic and hostile behaviors in the workplace will live in a community and interface with others outside of the workspace. Privacy laws and policies regarding external notifications may present unique challenges, particularly if adverse action (such as suspension, exclusion, or termination) is taken against the employee. While protecting the personnel and assets of a corporation is a priority, effective threat management seeks to avoid "punting" the problem to another agency. Navigating information-sharing between stakeholders—while balancing a community's security needs with an individual's privacy rights—is a continuing challenge for threat assessment and corporate safety professionals.

3) The "outsider attacker." Independently of physical security and other "target-hardening" measures, how do threat assessment and management professionals detect and disrupt the outside offender who has no direct connection to the targeted workspace? The outsider offender may choose the facility based on its desirability, availability, and vulnerability, or based on a perceived philosophical or symbolic significance. Are there any opportunities to develop awareness of hostile intent from an outsider attacker before the shooting begins? Do any pre-attack behaviors exist that can be observed and exploited for early detection? These questions are among the most difficult for a threat management team (TMT) to answer.

Despite the seemingly dark and difficult threatscape, there is cause for hope. A dedicated and growing force of threat assessment and threat management professionals continue to quietly work each day on TMTs to detect and disrupt acts of targeted workplace violence. These behind-the-scenes professionals prevent attacks, keep their employees and offices safe, and move offenders off a trajectory toward violence and on to a more positive pathway. The authors of *Workplace Violence: Issues in Threat Management*—Dr. Carri Casteel, Mr. Eugene Rugala, Mr. David

Bixler, and Ms. Christina M. Holbrook—are such professionals. They are published researchers, skilled practitioners, and innovative thought-leaders in this effort and have been advancing the tradecraft of threat assessment and management for corporate security for years.

I have had the great honor of learning many valuable lessons on workplace violence from this talented team, and in particular have benefitted from the mentorship of Gene Rugala. In 2002, while Gene was employed as a supervisory special agent with the FBI's Behavioral Analysis Unit, he and his colleagues hosted a threat assessment symposium featuring experts from public and private sectors. This collaboration led to the publication of the incredibly useful and still relevant monograph titled *Workplace Violence: Issues in Response*, of which Gene was the primary editor. To this day, I frequently open my well-worn copy of this operationally friendly document for guidance and direction. Anyone involved in the prevention of violence in the workplace will undoubtedly be familiar with Gene and his legacy of outstanding prevention efforts over decades, both with the FBI and beyond. Gene has also been a long-time member of the Association of Threat Assessment Professionals (ATAP), a non-profit organization that brings together law enforcement, mental health, and security professionals who seek to detect and disrupt acts of targeted violence. Gene's leadership in ATAP, particularly in the Washington, DC area, has stimulated information-sharing between agencies and progressive thinking on prevention efforts in truly meaningful ways.

Similarly, authors Dr. Carri Casteel, David Bixler, and Christina M. Holbrook each bring a wealth of experience and initiative to this book. Dr. Casteel's scholarship and research at the University of North Carolina Chapel Hill's Department of Epidemiology and now at the University of Iowa's Department of Environmental and Occupational Health has focused on workplace violence, particularly as it impacts retail, small business, and healthcare industries. Mr. Bixler and Ms. Holbrook have been active professionals on Boeing Corporation's TMT for years and truly understand the operational needs and pressures that come with protecting a large workforce within a major corporation.

Developing a multi-layered, system-wide approach for preventing workplace violence requires the use of holistic, agile, and defensible assessment and management strategies. To their credit, the authors of *Workplace Violence: Issues in Threat Management* offer such strategies here for the benefit of readers who seek to implement thoughtful and deliberate measures to prevent violence. Rather than myopically focus on one aspect of workplace violence, the authors have elegantly assembled a rich compendium that describes the key foundations and components involved in a workplace violence mitigation *system*. Recognizing that any threat management protocol must exist as part of a broader workplace violence prevention program, the authors have crafted an in-depth road map for companies who are initiating or updating their own policies and procedures. A review of operational/behavioral detection and disruption strategies is complemented by a discussion of pragmatic issues related to building and sustaining a successful workplace violence prevention program. Simultaneously comprehensive and detailed, *Workplace Violence: Issues in Threat Management* also covers nuts-and-bolts topics such as using a scalable and idiosyncratic development approach during the early planning phases of a violence prevention program; demonstrating non-traditional accomplishments to executive management (where the absence of an event is a success) for return on investment measurement; the role of fitness for duty examinations; and the importance of vigilant record keeping.

As a counterbalance to the daunting challenge of facing the new threatscape, *Workplace Violence: Issues in Threat Management* offers a thoughtful approach; namely, an intelligent and innovative method for creating a system that effectively leverages threat assessment and management resources in a corporate environment. Faced with the evolving dangers of targeted violence, this offering of the authors' collective wisdom and experience becomes an essential antidote and tool for corporate security stakeholders. Whether you are an experienced safety professional or new to this field, I am convinced that this book will quickly become one of your "go to" resources on the shelf, lined with tabbed flags and Post-Its™ sticking out of pages that glow with yellow highlights.

Workplace Violence: Issues in Threat Management represents some of the most current and best thinking on the topic of targeted workplace violence prevention. As you read and use this important guide, remember that there are many employees, customers, and families who are counting on you to detect and disrupt the violence before it occurs. This is an enormous responsibility and privilege, one that demands our collective attention, energy, and collaboration. Effective threat assessment and management thrives on the dynamic interplay between academia and industry and between research and operations, each informing the other and all evolving along the way. The authors of this book have given us a great opportunity to enhance our skills and stimulate our thinking, but most importantly, they have offered a plan for action. Through this book, they have provided a great service by reminding us that targeted workplace violence can be prevented and new headlines can be written …

"Today a plot to attack a local business was discovered and the shooting was thwarted before it occurred. No injuries were reported."

Andre Simons
Certified Threat Manager
ATAP Member
Supervisory Special Agent, FBI

The opinions expressed in this Foreword are solely those of the author and do not reflect the official position, opinions, or endorsement of the Federal Bureau of Investigation, the U.S. Department of Justice, or the United States Government.

Preface

Workplace violence is one of the leading causes of workplace death and traumatic injury, and employers in the United States have identified security and violence prevention as one of their top three business priorities. The overall cost of a workplace violence event to American business exceeds 35 million dollars, and costs to all parties exceed 4.2 billion dollars annually.[1]

Workplace violence can take many forms: violence between employees, violence from customers or clients, violence due to personal relationships such as domestic violence/stalking, and violence from crimes such as robberies. How can a company prepare for so many different types of threats, and what can a company do when a potentially violent situation is identified?

The foundation for preventing violent events is to identify problems early and to have a system in place to respond. The risk for violence is fairly small for most businesses, but the potential for threats from multiple sources is ever-present, and thus, businesses are challenged to have the right expertise without over-committing resources and personnel. Many companies have implemented threat management or threat assessment teams (TMTs/TATs) to bring together the right personnel to respond to complicated threat situations. For the purpose of this book, we will use "TMT" to describe both a TMT and a TAT. These teams consist of individuals from a variety of disciplines, for example, security, human resources, the employee assistance program, and legal and other ad hoc members. The members of this group convene when threatening behavior or a threat is brought to their attention. They assess the level of risk posed by the individual regarding the potential for violence. They also develop intervention strategies to mitigate or lower the level of risk. While the development of a threat management protocol is important, it must be part of an overall workplace violence prevention program with a policy, procedures, and processes to deal with these matters in an efficient and effective way, coupled with education and awareness of all managers and employees as to what role they play in the prevention of violence.

In this book we will define what workplace violence is, the myths and realities, the latest statistics and thinking in the prevention of workplace violence, and how companies can develop a comprehensive threat management program. Additional perspectives will be provided by guest authors who are subject matter experts in employment law and domestic/intimate partner violence. Actual case studies will highlight important points and will educate both novices and experienced practitioners in the development of a prevention program. The final highlight will be one company's experience in developing and implementing a workplace violence prevention program. While this company is a large multinational corporation, its program can be emulated by small and medium-sized organizations, which will be discussed in this book.

While there have been many books that have examined this subject, this book will provide the latest thinking in prevention, threat assessment, and intervention. This book can serve as a reference guide to be used by security, human resources, and other professionals tasked with creating a workplace violence prevention program. It will allow these professionals to take this guide and develop or enhance their own program, which incorporates the experience and lessons learned from individuals involved in workplace violence research, program development, and threat assessment and intervention.

Note

1 Peek-Asa, Corinne, Casteel, Carri, Rugala, Eugene A., Romano, S., Ramirez, M., Workplace violence investigations and activation of the threat management teams in a multinational corporation, *Journal of Occupational and Environmental Medicine* (July 2013).

Acknowledgments

To Dr. Lynn Jenkins, who was taken from us prematurely, a pioneer and leader in the workplace violence prevention field working with the National Institute for Occupational Safety and Health (NIOSH); she was a colleague and a friend and is missed by all who knew her.

The authors would like to acknowledge, with appreciation and gratitude, many colleagues and threat assessment professionals, who are too numerous to mention in this ever-growing threat management field. It has been the opportunity of a lifetime to work with such incredible and talented people, who have shaped our views and contributed greatly to the field of threat assessment and management.

A special thank you to our expert contributing authors, Andre Simons, Pamela A. Paziotopoulos, Michael A. Crane, and Matthew W. Doherty. Their expertise added greatly to this book.

Finally, we could not do this without the support of our families and loved ones. Their love, understanding, and encouragement allowed us to dedicate our time and pursue our passion in this challenging field.

1 Introduction

What Is Workplace Violence?

In 2011, ASIS International (ASIS) and the Society of Human Resource Management (SHRM) completed a yearlong endeavor and produced a document, based on the American National Standard model, entitled *Workplace Violence Prevention and Intervention*. This standard dealt with an issue that has long plagued America's workplaces, that is, violence that occurs in the workplace setting. A multi-disciplinary group of individuals representing human resources, security, law enforcement, mental health, and the law, from private industry and government, put their collective heads together to document the latest thinking and "best practices" for the prevention and mitigation of this type of violence.

This group defined workplace violence as *A spectrum of behaviors, including overt acts of violence, threats, and other conduct, that generates a reasonable concern for the safety from violence, where a nexus exists between the behavior and the physical safety of employees and others (such as customers, clients and business associates) on site, or off-site when related to the organization.*[1] Others, including the Federal Bureau of Investigation (FBI) in *Workplace Violence: Issues in Response* (2004), define workplace violence as *any action that may threaten the safety of an employee, impact an employee's physical or psychological well-being, or cause damage to company property.*[2] The Occupational Safety and Health Administration (OSHA), in its bulletin dated September 8, 2011 entitled *Enforcement Procedures for Investigating or Inspecting Workplace Violence Incidents*, utilizes a definition from the National Institute for Occupational Safety and Health (NIOSH), part of the Centers for Disease Control (CDC), as *violent acts (including physical assaults and threats of assaults) directed toward persons at work or on duty.*[3]

Regardless of whose definition you use, workplace violence in all its forms is a serious and continuing issue confronting workplaces not only in the United States but around the world. While most people think of workplace violence as sensational multiple homicides perpetrated by disgruntled current or former employees, workplace violence is much more that. Homicide and other physical assaults fall on a spectrum or continuum that also includes threatening behavior and threats, domestic violence that spills over into the workplace, stalking behavior, bullying, intimidation, all forms of harassment, and other forms of conduct which create a climate of fear and distrust in the workplace.[4]

Workplace violence is a recognized risk and occupational hazard in some occupations (e.g., law enforcement); however, in most other occupations, it is often an unexpected hazard. The potential for this type of violence can be minimized if appropriate prevention procedures to address the possibility of violence are put in place within an organization. These procedures will be discussed in more detail in subsequent chapters.

Perception versus Reality

While media attention and the general public are focused on acts of mass murder that seemingly occur every day at a workplace somewhere in America, these catastrophic acts

Reasons Workplace Violence Occurs	*Perpetrators Of Workplace Violence*	
• Work-related conflict • Personal conflict • Domestic violence • Robbery • Revenge for being fired, laid off, or passed over for promotion • Angry customer, client supplier, or patient • Obsessed stalker • Terrorism	• Employees • Former employees • Temporary or part–time employees • Contractors • Customers	• Suppliers • Clients • Patients • Acquaintances of employees • Family members of employees • Strangers • Terrorists

Figures 1.1 and 1.2 Reasons for Workplace Violence and Who Are the Perpetrators

of violence are actually quite infrequent and rare. In fact, workplace homicides have been on the decline for years, dropping by over 50% as indicated by 2016 statistics supplied by the U.S. Department of Labor, Census of Fatal Occupational Injuries (CFOI), which comes out every year, detailing fatal injuries among all occupations in U.S. industry and government. Managers are most likely to deal with threatening behavior and/or threats, intimidation, bullying, domestic violence and stalking, and other forms of abusive behavior that will likely never lead to homicide.

Another perception is that most workplace homicides are the result of a disgruntled employee on a mission of revenge for some perceived wrong perpetrated by a fellow co-worker or manager, and wanting to get even, or perhaps a domestic violence situation that spills over into a workplace. While this might be true in some cases, the vast majority of workplace homicides are perpetrated by strangers and happen during robberies and related criminal activity. In fact, studies have shown that certain occupations are more at risk for this type of physical violence to occur. These occupations are in retail, law enforcement, and the medical profession. Research has identified risk factors that could be applicable to each of these occupations. Some of these are: working with the public or volatile, unstable people; working alone or in isolated areas; handling money and valuables; providing services and care; and working where alcohol is served. Other factors, such as time of day and location, may also be contributory.

Categories of Workplace Violence

OSHA/NIOSH workplace typology[5] classifies workplace violence incidents according to the relationship between the perpetrator and the victim or target, and to the organization. This typology incorporates four categories or types of workplace violence:

> **Type 1 Criminal Intent:** Violent acts by people who enter the workplace to commit a robbery or other crime—or current or former employees who enter the workplace with the intent to commit a crime.
>
> **Type 2 Customer/Client/Patients:** Violence directed at employees by customers, clients, patients, students, inmates, or any others to whom the employer provides a service.
>
> **Type 3 Co-worker:** Violence against co-workers, supervisors, or managers by a current or former employee, supervisor, or manager.
>
> **Type 4 Personal:** Violence in the workplace by someone who does not work there, but who is known to, or has a personal relationship with, an employee.

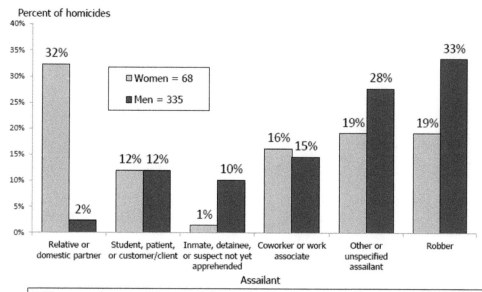

Figure 1.3 Percentage of Work-Related Homicides by Gender of Decedent and Assailant Type, 2016
Note: Percentages may not add to 100 due to rounding.
Source: United States Bureau of Labor Statistics (2017).

Workplace violence can occur anytime and anywhere. Even with the best of prevention programs, an organization can never eliminate the threat of some type of violent act occurring. However, the threat of violence can be reduced if problematic behavior is reported and/or identified early and dealt with in an appropriate manner.

Many organizations have put in place policy and procedures to deal with the possibility of violence; however, even with some of the high-profile incidents that have occurred, many still lack the ability to deal with this issue. These organizations believe in some of the myths often expressed as to why a program should not be developed or put in place. Some of these myths include: "it can't/won't happen here," "we are all professionals and should all get along," "most situations will resolve themselves if given enough time," to name a few; however, we know that no one and no organization is immune to this type of behavior.

How many times after a violent incident, typically a shooting perpetrated by a problematic employee, do co-workers when interviewed by law enforcement and/or the media report that the perpetrator "snapped," or that the violent act occurred "out of the blue," that the employer "never saw it coming"? Conversely, others who knew the offender might say, "if anyone was going to bring a gun into the workplace and start shooting it was him," or "I have been scared that something like this would happen." Research and experience in dealing with these violent crime issues suggest that no one "snaps," that no individual decides one day to come into work with a gun to shoot his manager or co-workers for no apparent reason. While it may not be known at the time what drove an individual to commit a violent act, typically, once a thorough investigation is conducted, behaviors of concern become known, but no one was able to see the developing situation in its entirety and to "connect the dots." Warning

Figure 1.4 Pathway to Violence
Source: Calhoun and Weston (2003).

signs were missed or discounted, and as a result whatever grievance the individual had was left unaddressed, and violence was the result. There may be other situations where motivation is never determined, as it is something only the offender knows. In many of these cases, the offender takes his/her own life, thus leaving everyone to ask the question "Why?". What we do know is that there is a pathway to violence, one that is evolutionary and builds over time. Many times, threats or inappropriate comments are made to colleagues or co-workers, but they are not reported to anyone, as there is a belief that the individual did not mean it or was just blowing off some steam. This is what is termed as "leakage" (for a full explanation see Chapter 4): comments made by an individual to a third party about what he or she would like to do, what he or she is planning to do. There might be other behaviors of concern or warning signs, which, when looked at in totality, might have suggested the possibility of future violence.

Figure 1.4 represents the pathway to violence.[6]

Conditions That Can Lead to Violence

Researchers and other experts agree that violence is more likely to happen in workplaces that fail to properly screen their employees, for example; do not perform security background checks (e.g., credit or criminal checks) of all new employees and periodically re-check current ones; lack policies or procedures to deal with the possibility of a violent event occurring in the workplace; do not provide proper training to managers and employees in how to deal with this issue, so that they ignore warning signs and/or fail to manage; tolerate bullying and other forms of harassment that create an environment which is toxic; subject employees to frequent change and uncertainty; and fail to treat employees with dignity, respect, and compassion. These factors, combined with individual or personal issues, often combine to create a volatile mix.

Lessons learned from violent situations that have occurred in the past in workplaces throughout the United States and abroad suggest that organizations should have in place some type of workplace violence prevention program to deal with threatening behavior and threats, and the possibility that a violent act could occur: anything from a physical assault to a homicide.

ASIS/SHRM, the FBI, and other organizations that have studied this issue suggest that organizations must have a top-down, multi-disciplinary approach to deal with the possibility of violence. Managers and employees have to become stakeholders in their own safety and security, as the responsibility for a safe working environment does not fall exclusively on the shoulders of security and/or human resources, but is everyone's responsibility. The chief executive officer/chief security officer (CEO/CSO) has to emphasize to employees that violence prevention, employee safety, and promoting a safe working environment is his or her top priority. Additionally, a policy defining workplace violence, what constitutes prohibited behaviors, and procedures to address reports of concerns has to be put in place to deal with these issues. A threat management process, which we will explore in great detail in subsequent chapters, is paramount. A multi-disciplinary team, consisting of representatives from security, human resources, the employee assistance program, and legal as well as other ad hoc members as needed, such as management, ethics, and employee relations, should come together to evaluate reports of threatening behavior and threats, which are categorized, investigated, and tracked. There should be an employee assistance program for referrals for fitness for duty or threat assessment by an external forensic psychologist, and/or any other issues where counseling may be required. There should be appropriate disciplinary procedures, which are consistent and fair. Most important to this whole endeavor is the training of managers and employees, raising their awareness of this issue, recognizing potential warning signs, and how to report so there is a greater likelihood that problematic behavior will be reported and addressed. Many times, we have seen these problematic behaviors not addressed by management, and they escalate to an assault or some other violent event.

The foundation for preventing violence at work is to identify problems early and to have a system in place to respond. The risk for violence is fairly small for most businesses, but the potential for threats from multiple sources is ever-present, and thus, businesses are challenged to have the right expertise without over-committing resources and personnel. Organizations have formed multi-disciplinary threat management teams (TMTs) to bring together the right personnel to respond to complicated threat situations. These teams consist of individuals from a variety of disciplines; for example, security, human resources, the employee assistance program, and legal. The members of this group convene when threatening behavior or a threat is brought to their attention, and they assess the level of risk posed by the individual regarding the potential for violence. They also develop intervention strategies to mitigate or lower the level of risk.

In subsequent chapters, we will deal with the elements of an effective program and talk about threatening behavior and threats, and the management of such threats as well as intervention and response. We will speak about an issue which many organizations are trying to deal with, domestic or intimate partner violence and stalking and its impact on the workplace, the role of employee assistance programs, and legal considerations in dealing with threatening behavior and threats. Additionally, we will talk about one organization's experience in putting together a "Best in Class" workplace violence prevention program and the "trials and tribulations" it went through to get buy-in, to train, and to maintain that program at a high level so that eventual complacency would not creep in. Finally, case examples will highlight and reinforce some of the concepts we will discuss.

Notes

1. Speer, R., and contributors, *Workplace Violence Prevention and Intervention*, American National Standard, Alexandria, VA: ASIS International (2011).
2. Rugala, E.A., Isaacs, A. *Workplace Violence: Issues in Response*, Critical Incident Response Group, National Center for the Analysis of Violent Crime, FBI Academy, Quantico, VA (2004).
3. OSHA, National Institute for Occupational Safety and Health (NIOSH), *Enforcement Procedures for Investigating or Inspecting Workplace Violence Incidents*, Washington, DC (September, 2011).
4. Ibid., *supra* note 2.
5. NIOSH, *Violence in the Workplace, Risk Factors and Prevention Strategies*, Washington, DC (1996).
6. Calhoun, F.S., Weston, S.W., *Contemporary Threat Management: A Practical Guide for Identifying, Assessing and Managing Individuals of Violent Intent*, San Diego, CA: Specialized Training Services (2003).

2 The Foundation
Creation of a Workplace Violence Prevention Policy

It is essential for companies to have an approved written workplace violence prevention policy in place. It will be the foundation for your threat management program.

Your policy should be written by a multi-disciplinary team (e.g., members from security, human resources, legal, and employee assistance program) to obtain each group's buy-in. From a legal perspective, there should be only one policy, with overarching requirements and responsibilities, in place for your entire company. This is important from the legal perspective, and will eliminate any confusion and ensure consistency.

It should be reviewed on a regular schedule (we recommend every three years, or sooner, if needed) to ensure it remains current; it should be communicated to all employees and should be readily accessible (i.e., in a centralized repository).

The policy should be approved by your company's chief security officer or someone who has the authority to mandate these requirements throughout your company.

Leadership buy-in will help to ensure that responsibilities and requirements are clearly communicated to employees. The latter is critical in case your company is ever faced with legal ramifications when questioned: "Did your company do its due diligence when assessing and responding to workplace violence incidents?"

When creating your policy for the first time, be prepared for some pushback from those who might not understand the importance of this program. This is the time to help educate your executive leadership on what is happening within your company, in your community, and nationally. Many leaders want to believe that this could not happen at their company. Unfortunately, it does: from a verbal communicated threat to physical assaults. The goal is to catch these events early, while they are a low-level risk. Maintaining metrics on threat management cases is extremely helpful and can empirically inform leadership on what is happening within your company. We will cover maintaining metrics in a subsequent chapter.

Many companies today do business both domestically and internationally, and each country may have varying laws; however, this does not mean you need a policy for each country. Rather, a thorough understanding of the nuances in each country to ensure your company is in compliance with them is needed.

Each company's policy should be tailored to the company's organizational structure. For example, not all companies have a security department. In this case, the responsibility for security may fall to someone in the human resources or facilities department, who may have little or no security background and may count on local law enforcement to provide assistance. Others may use an outside subject matter expert to provide advice on cases and to help develop a mitigation plan. Remember, one size does not fit all. Your policy should be scalable. What is best for your company might not be best for another.

Use caution when including terminology such as "zero tolerance" in your policy. Zero tolerance puts your company in the position of acting on every allegation that is made and imposing automatic discipline even if there was no merit to the allegation. Zero tolerance policies do not allow your company to exercise discretion or change directions to fit the facts and circumstances surrounding the incident; they are designed to impose a pre-determined discipline regardless of individual culpability, the circumstances, or past history. Instead of using the terminology "zero tolerance," it might be better to state: "all incidents are taken seriously and are thoroughly investigated." This will allow your company to assess the facts and circumstances on a case-by-case basis and then determine the best course of action and appropriate corrective action.

What should be included in your policy? The following list provides some elements to consider including in your company policy, ensuring that they align with your business structure.

- **Title of Your Program.** Give careful consideration to what you want to name your program. Should it be "Workplace Violence Prevention Program," "Maintaining a Safe and Secure Environment," or "Threat Management Program"? Think about the message you are sending your employees when you are selecting a name
- **Date of Release.** We recommend establishing a frequency (annually, every three years) for reviewing your company policy
- **Policy Number.** We recommend establishing a sequential numbering system to keep track of what policies are in place
- **Purpose of Policy.** Address what your policy will include, such as "The policy establishes a process to identify, assess, respond to, mitigate, and monitor threatening behavior, threats and acts of violence in the workplace and includes associated training and education." If your policy covers both U.S. and non-U.S. locations, consider adding a disclaimer regarding this, such as "if the controlling local law conflicts with a provision of this policy, management should instruct affected personnel, in writing, on the methods for complying with controlling local law or customer requirements"
- **Applies to Section.** This section would cover the applicability across the company (e.g., Enterprise writing)
- **Authority Reference, if Applicable.** If your company has a structured approach to writing—for example, policy, procedure, process—then your threat management program should have a reference to that higher-authority writing. In essence, what gives an organization the authority to write and release writings within your company?
- **Approved by.** Identify the executive who is ultimately responsible for your company's policy. This could be your company's chief security officer or director of Human Resources
- **Definitions.** Do not presume that your employees understand the various terminology used throughout the policy. Key definitions can include, but are not limited to, Threat, Threatening Behavior, Acts of Violence, Course of Conduct, Active Shooter, Workplace (would include virtual workers and employees on company business), and Threat Management Team
- **Policy Objectives.** Outline the objectives of your company's policy. What type of environment is your company trying to establish, such as a "safe and secure workplace environment"? What do you want your employees and management to be aware of, such as "potential warning signs and how and when to report them"?
- **Requirements.** This section can address the formation and composition of threat management teams (TMTs); frequency of how often TMTs should meet; tools these teams should use to document incidents; requirements on how to manage threats; and education and communication requirements regarding your threat management prevention program
- **Responsibilities.** Specific responsibilities for not only each discipline (e.g., security, human resources, the employee assistance program, legal, ethics) on the TMT, but also employees and managers

- **Related Material.** Additional materials that would support your company's policy, such as a drug and alcohol program, a corrective action policy, a weapons policy, and links to educational materials for your workforce

Whatever your company comes up with, ensure it is clear, concise, and actionable. Your policy should be in writing and should be reviewed and updated regularly. It should be communicated to your employees so that they know your company has a policy and what their responsibilities are for recognizing and reporting incidents.

3 Development of a Threat Management Program

You have probably heard or read by now that "the best prevention is early intervention." These are not just words; they are critical to the success of your program. In order to identify, assess, respond to, mitigate, and monitor threatening behavior and threats in the workplace early in the progression of the behavior, you must have a proactive program.

Think about why fire prevention programs are so successful. These programs are designed with an 80/20 rule in mind: 80% prevention and 20% response. A strong threat management program should be designed in the same manner.

In our last chapter, we talked about your company policy being the foundation of your program. In this chapter, we will now go into depth on the elements of a comprehensive threat management program. This chapter will cover:

- Designing a program that is scalable to your company's infrastructure and needs
- Forming and training a threat management team (TMT)
- Categorizing threat management incidents
- Record keeping (intake and case management)
- Maintaining threat management metrics
- Taking proper preventive action by educating managers in threat management processes and heightening employees' awareness and general knowledge of your program
- Preparing and responding to advanced threat incidents

Designing a Program

When designing your threat management program, think about your company and its infrastructure: small-size, mid-size, or large-size company; domestic or international, or both; union or non-union workforce, or both; includes a contract labor force; resident customers at your site; work environment is a factory, office, retail, or combination. All of these need to be taken into consideration and designed into your program. We recommend benchmarking with companies that have a program already in place and are similar in size and complexity. Include key disciplines in the design—such as security (specializing in threat assessment), the law department, health services/employee assistance program (EAP), human resources, and employee relations if your company has a union base. This gives everyone ownership in your program—a voice—and therefore, a comprehensive identification of gaps and solutions you can work out together. Be prepared for road blocks. Some companies' executive leadership might think that a program is not needed. You might even hear "Everyone gets along" and "There has never been an incident." Designing a program before an incident should ever occur is a wise investment. Ensuring your employees come to work in a safe and secure workplace environment is what every company strives for. Hopefully, your company will never have to use your program's guidance, but should an incident occur, your company would be prepared to identify, access, respond to, mitigate, and monitor the incident.

Once your program is designed, continually look at ways for improving it. It should not be designed and then put on a shelf.

Formation of a Threat Management Team (TMT)

Many companies have implemented threat management teams (TMTs) to bring together the right personnel who can respond to and mitigate threatening behavior, threats, and acts of violence, and some research has examined threat management approaches to consider implementing at your company.

TMTs include members from multiple disciplines (for example, security, human resources, health services, the EAP, and the law department) within an organization who work together to reduce threatening behaviors, threats, and acts of violence and their consequences. One of their primary roles is to identify, investigate, and respond to potential threats (Rugala and Isaacs, 2004; ASIS SHRM, 2011).

TMTs can also play an important role in primary prevention, such as providing training to managers and employees, establishing outreach programs with local law enforcement and other agencies, and helping to establish a workplace culture that is respectful and encourages open communication. From a response perspective, having a team that works well together is critical to success. For example, the members need to be familiar with each other's expertise and respect each other's contribution. Additionally, they all need to know how the company's policies and procedures define how the response process should be administered. Once a company has identified the individuals who have responsibility for responding to threatening behavior, threats, and acts of violence, the team needs to be trained in carrying out an organized and cohesive response.

Each team member is critical to the success of your program. Documenting their roles and responsibilities on the TMT is essential. Sample responsibilities include:

Security
- Serve as the TMT leader and ensure that TMT meetings are held on a regular basis and that meetings and incidents are appropriately documented
- Determine when to convene the team to assess, respond to, monitor, and mitigate threatening behavior, threats, and acts of violence
- Be familiar with processes for responding to threatening behavior, threats, and acts of violence; respond appropriately when violence is threatened or occurs within the workplace and assist in restoring order; complete initial incident reports and debrief on incidents as appropriate
- Assign trained investigators to participate on the TMT
- Identify outside resources (e.g., within the local law enforcement community, emergency services) to be able to assist if an incident should occur and their immediate support is needed
- Immediately notify key management of all significant cases
- Distribute threat management program information, training, and resources to company personnel
- Coordinate requests for surveillance and requests for external professional experts for consultation or training (e.g., threat assessment, domestic (intimate partner) violence)

Human Resources
- Contact security when advised of a threatening behavior, threat, or act of violence in the workplace
- Assist in referral to EAP, as appropriate, for employees who are placed on administrative leave pending investigation and who are required to have a Fitness for Duty EAP evaluation prior to returning to work

- For employees advised that EAP evaluation will be a condition of employment, secure an employee signature on a Release of Information form, allowing EAP vendors to communicate with your company about the employee's return-to-work clearance status

Health Services/EAP

- Contact security when advised of a threat to the workplace as allowed by law and professional standards
- Identify, where available, resources in communities who are trained and available to assist the company in the event of a threat management incident. These resources will include specialists who have expertise in threatening behavior, threats, and acts of violence
- Assess employees sent to Health Services/EAP and refer them, when indicated, to appropriate medical providers
- Act as a liaison with community provider(s) who will evaluate and, if needed, provide treatment to an employee following a threat or act of violence
- Determine whether an employee who is referred to Health Services/EAP after exhibiting threatening behavior, threats, or act of violence is fit for duty before the employee returns to the workplace
- Provide counseling, referral, support, participation, and assistance in the coordination of threat management incident debriefings for and in conjunction with the TMT, as appropriate

Law Department

- Provide legal counsel and related support to TMTs in responding to and preventing threatening behavior, threats, and acts of violence in the workplace, as needed
- Report all threatening behavior, threats, and acts of violence to security and a human resources representative as soon as possible

Providing your TMTs with the proper tools and resources is critical to your program. These resources include a threat management team guide (outlining each member's roles and responsibilities in detail), a threat assessment evaluation intake (documentation, documentation, documentation is so critical), and a threat management case evaluation tool.

Companies should consider using or designing threat management assessment and response matrices, which help guide the TMT's decisions when an incident occurs. They should be used as screening tools, not diagnostic instruments, to assist the TMT in identifying an incident as a low-, medium-, or high-level risk. These tools should only be used by the TMT professionals in a team meeting so that the level of threat can be assessed by a multi-disciplinary group. These tools should also be used with the understanding that the analysis and prediction of violence relies not only on the personality of the individual being assessed but also on the effect of uncontrollable, unpredictable, and/or unknown events which may have occurred, or may be occurring, in an individual's life. Environmental changes, medication use, alcohol consumption, drug use, medical issues, and personal conflicts can all affect the thought process of an individual and may be factors in how to respond to an incident.

Prediction of violence is neither a reliable nor an exact science. The assessment is based upon probabilities, noting, however, that no two acts or personalities are exactly alike. An assessment is based solely on the facts and information provided through investigation. An assessment could be modified or changed should further investigation into the matter invalidate the original facts on which an assessment was based. It is difficult to predict future behavior with any degree of certainty. However, it may be possible to identify and address the existence of certain elements or criteria which should elevate prudent concern for potential severity.

When developing a threat management assessment and response matrices, consider addressing the following:

- Assessment Matrix (e.g., examples of threatening behaviors, threats and acts of violence; possession of/access to/use of weapons; personal behaviors of concern; history of violence and conflict)
- Mitigating Factors (examples of what can potentially reduce the level of risk; for example, remorse for actions and/or inappropriate behaviors)
- Organizational Influences (examples of what can potentially increase the level of risk; for example, management tolerance of inappropriate behavior of workgroup)
- Insider Threat (extremely important element to include if you have employees or other business partners who have or had authorized access to an organization's network, system, or data and intentionally exceeded or misused that access in a manner that negatively affected the confidentiality, integrity, use, or availability of the organization's information or information systems)
- Domestic Violence (Intimate Partner) Information and Behavior (outline the impact on the workplace and identify the behaviors of concern; offer safety planning tips)
- Stalking Information and Behavior (outline the impact on the workplace and identify the behaviors of concern; offer safety planning tips)
- Response Matrix (outline each discipline's roles and responsibilities)

The foundation for mitigating threatening behaviors, threats, and act of violence is to identify problems early in the process and to have a system in place to respond. The risk for imminent violent situations is fairly small for most businesses, but the potential for threats from internal or external sources exists for all businesses. Thus, businesses are challenged to have the right expertise without over-committing resources and personnel.

Another tool to consider designing and using is a threat management case evaluation tool. After an incident, the TMT should consider evaluating the process and identify lessons learned—pre incident, incident, and post incident. It is through this process that improvements can be made, if needed, to ensure the effectiveness of your threat management program and assess how well the TMT worked together.

- **Pre-Incident Assessment Focus**: Prior knowledge of concerning issues and/or subject
- **Incident Assessment Focus:** Assessing the TMT overall; team dynamics
- **Post-Incident Assessment Focus:** Lessons learned; where can improvements be made, if any

There follow some sample questions for each focus area:

Analysis of the Pre-Incident—*Looking back at the incident, what could have been done differently?*
- Did the TMT have any prior knowledge on this subject/offender? [] Yes [] No
- Was information on the incident provided to the TMT members in advance of the meeting? [] Yes [] No

- Was there enough information for the TMT to review to accurately assess the situation?
  - Past behaviors of concern
  - Criminal records
  - Work history, to include performance issues; any corrective action
  - Interviews of co-workers, management, and victim
  - To determine the risk level as a TMT

Analysis of the Incident—*Looking back at the incident, what could have been done differently?*

- What are some observations that the TMT leader observed and should share with the entire TMT?
- Were TMT members easily contacted?
- Were members able to convene quickly? By what means did that occur?
- If the primary TMT member was not available, were their backups available?
- Where and how was the meeting held?

Analysis of the Post-Incident—*Looking back at the incident, what could have been done differently?*

- Was EAP engaged for post-stress debriefing resources/availability?
  - Victim(s) [] Yes [] No
  - Witness(es) [] Yes [] No
  - TMT members [] Yes [] No
  - First Responders [] Yes [] No
  - Workgroup [] Yes [] No
- Case management. Has the TMT followed up on this incident since it occurred? [] Yes [] No

Importance of Categorizing Threat Management Incidents

We cannot stress enough the importance of categorizing your threat management incidents. Start with identifying categories based on behaviors; for example, abnormal behavior, assault, battery, communicated threat, domestic violence, homicide, possession of a weapon, stalking, suicidal ideation, and suicide. Then define each type of behavior so that everyone will have a clear understanding of what each means. Note that incidents can be categorized with more than one behavior, or you may choose to categorize the incident based on the most severe behavior.

There should be no "other" category. It will not help when working a case and trying to describe the person's behavior. Think about trying to describe the incident and saying, "the subject exhibited 'other' behavior." It may sound funny, but in reality it could come across that you do not know what behavior the person exhibited. In addition, it forces you to select a behavior which your threat management program has guidelines to address. Here are some example definitions for the behaviors identified earlier:

- **Abnormal Behavior:** Causes discomfort to others, deviation from typical patterns and actions, demonstrating emotions of concern
- **Assault:** Any willful attempt or threat to inflict injury upon another person, when coupled with an apparent present ability to do so, or a show of force that creates a reasonable expectation of bodily harm

- **Battery:** Intentionally or recklessly causing offensive physical contact or bodily harm performed against a victim, which is not consented to by the victim. Can be with hands, body, or other mechanism (e.g., water bottle, book, tool)
- **Communicated Threat:** An expression of an intention to injure another person made verbally, in writing, by gesture, or by electronic means
- **Domestic Violence:** Violence committed by one family member, spouse, former spouse, or household member against another
- **Homicide:** The killing of a human being by another
- **Possession of a Weapon:** The possession of any instrument or device designed, modified, displayed, or used with intent to do bodily harm. This includes functional firearms and other prohibited weapons
- **Stalking:** The act of repeatedly following or harassing another person in circumstances that would cause a reasonable person to fear for his/her safety
- **Suicidal Ideation:** Thoughts of suicide, wishes to die
- **Suicide:** The act or attempt of killing oneself

Record Keeping (Intake and Case Management)

One of the most critical elements of your program will be how you document the incident. A data gathering tool, such as a threat assessment evaluation/intake form, will help immensely. This evaluation/intake assessment should be completed for each incident and by the TMT leader or designee. When completed, a copy of this evaluation/intake should be retained in your company's investigative system, where it can be used for future reference or to support an internal and/or external legal request. The evaluation/intake should cover items such as:

- Who Was Involved? (Victim, subject, witness)
- When and What Happened? (provide as much detail and specificity as possible)
- Threat Management *Primary* Behavior Categories?
- Threat Management *Secondary* Behavior Categories?
- Indicate Factors Involved (see examples in the threat assessment evaluation/intake form template provided in this chapter)
- Potential Warning Signs or Behaviors of Concern (identify any factors in the last 12 months)
- Initial Threat Assessment (e.g., low, medium, high)
- Action Plan Follow-Up with Department or Individual (identify all that apply)
- Actions Recommended and/or Taken to Manage the Threat/Subject (identify all that apply)
- TMT Members at Initial Meeting
- Disposition of the Incident
- Case Management Updates (provide as much details as possible)

Sample of what a threat assessment evaluation/intake may contain.

Metrics

Often metrics are defined as a "standard for measuring or evaluating something, especially one that uses figures or statistics" (Dictionary.com).

[INSERT COMPANY NAME] PROPRIETARY

Distribution limited to Threat Management Team members only (when completed)

Instructions: This evaluation/intake assessment should be completed by the Threat Management Team leader or designee. When completed a copy of this evaluation/intake should be added to the [Insert the Company's Tracking System Name].

I. Who Was Involved?	Reporting Party:	Date:	Phone:
Suspect(s) Involved: Check if suspect has a security clearance (see [Company Policy] for addl. instructions)	EMPLOYEE ID:	BU, Job Title & Shift:	Dept. & Bldg.:	Phone:
Victim(s) Involved:	EMPLOYEE ID:	BU, Job Title & Shift:	Dept. & Bldg.:	Phone:
Witness(s) Involved:	EMPLOYEE ID:	BU, Job Title & Shift:	Dept. & Bldg.:	Phone:
Others Involved:	EMPLOYEE ID:	BU, Job Title & Shift:	Dept. & Bldg.:	Phone:
II. When and What Happened?	Case Number:	Incident Date/Time/Location of Occurrence:	

Incident Details:

Figure 3.1 Threat Assessment Evaluation/Intake

IIIa. Threat Management Categories? (Check primary category; see definitions below; ensure this is identified in [Insert Company Tracking System Name])

Instructions on how to check boxes (electronic version): STEP 1 – Double click on box; STEP 2 – Click on "Checked"; STEP 3 – Click "OK"; Will automatically add the check to the box

Abnormal Behavior
- ☐ Assault
- ☐ Battery

- ☐ Communicated Threat
- ☐ Domestic Violence
- ☐ Homicide

- ☐ Possession of a weapon
- ☐ Stalking
- ☐ Suicide

- ☐ Suicidal Ideation

IIIb. Threat Management Categories? (Check secondary category(ies); see last page for definitions)

Abnormal Behavior
- ☐ Assault
- ☐ Battery

- ☐ Communicated Threat
- ☐ Domestic Violence
- ☐ Homicide

- ☐ Possession of a weapon
- ☐ Stalking
- ☐ Suicide

- ☐ Suicidal Ideation

IV. Indicate Factors Involved (Help to Determine Risk Level of Incident) (Check all that apply)

Low Risk	Medium Risk	High Risk	Extreme Risk
☐ Intimidating attitude or actions (e.g., bullying)	☐ Overt, covert, or indirect threats with increasing frequency and specificity	☐ Specific direct threats with increased frequency and intensity; evidence that a violent act will occur	**(NOTE:** *The Threat Management Assessment and Response Matrices is not for use for Extreme Risk situations; reference the Enterprise Advanced Threat Prevention and Response Standards.)*
☐ Perceived harassment or verbal abuse	☐ Weapon in vehicle on company property	☐ Intense anger or uncontrollable rage	
☐ Abusive behavior	☐ Attempts to instigate fights	☐ Any willful or unlawful use of force (battery) or violence upon another (e.g., grabbing, biting, grappling, hitting)	
☐ Excessive use of profanity	☐ Open defiance of rules	☐ Criminal stalking	
☐ Argumentative	☐ Vandalism or property theft	☐ Overt threats to fatally injure	
☐ Lack of cooperation upon request	☐ Feeling of persecution by others	☐ Possession of weapons	
☐ Sexual comments or gestures	☐ Sexual or violent notes sent to others	☐ Known substance abuse	
☐ Negative attitude toward rules	☐ Threats to harm oneself or others in the workplace	☐ Vandalism, sabotage, or intentional damage to company property	
☐ Disrespect for authority and/or management	☐ Intentional physical conduct (e.g., pushing, bumping, restriction of movement of another person)	☐ Suicide attempt	
☐ Firearm ownership	☐ Stalking behaviors	☐ Stays to themselves, perceived loner	
☐ Angry and volatile outbursts (e.g., assault, door slamming, throwing objects)	☐ Fascination with weapons/themes of revenge, expressed desire to harm others	☐ Violated protective order	
☐ Emotionally erratic	☐ Conscious intimidation or repeated bullying		
☐ Indirect or veiled threats	☐ Recent/pending corrective action, layoff, or poor performance review		
☐ Inappropriate use of computing and phone systems	☐ Substance abuse		
☐ Subject of an open investigation	☐ Active protective order		

V. Potential Warning Signs or Behaviors of Concern (Check any factors in the last 12 months.)

- ☐ Threatening behaviors
- ☐ Intimidation and bullying
- ☐ Demonstrating emotions of concern
- ☐ Angry and volatile outbursts
- ☐ Perceived persecution or victimization
- ☐ Obsession with an employee or manager
- ☐ Fascination with weapons and theme of revenge
- ☐ History of violence
- ☐ Possession of weapons
- ☐ Intense, uncontrollable rage
- ☐ Threatening or intimidating body language
- ☐ Communicated threats
- ☐ Persistent pursuit or stalking
- ☐ Threats to harm oneself and/or others in the workplace
- ☐ Substance abuse
- ☐ Other (specify) _____

VI. Initial Threat Assessment

- ☐ Low
- ☐ Medium
- ☐ High
- ☐ Extreme

VII. Action Plan Follow-Up With (Check all that apply):

- ☐ No further action
- ☐ Management Consultation
- ☐ Notified Enterprise TMT
- ☐ Health Services
- ☐ EAP
- ☐ HRG
- ☐ Security
- ☐ Law Dept.
- ☐ Law Enforcement
- ☐ Corp. Investigations
- ☐ HR Investigations
- ☐ Victim(s)
- ☐ Witness(es)
- ☐ Subject(s)
- ☐ Other (specify): _____

VIII. Actions recommended and/or taken to manage the threat/subject (Check all that apply):

- ☐ Continue monitoring subject
- ☐ Coach subject (HR, Mgmt or Security)
- ☐ Prepare / Release BOLO
- ☐ Activate "Do Not Badge or Admit" in EPSS
- ☐ Deactivate AMS
- ☐ Request Security Background Check via SBS organization
- ☐ Voluntary EAP referral
- ☐ Mandatory EAP referral
- ☐ Fitness for Duty evaluation
- ☐ Threat Assessment evaluation
- ☐ Notify Law Enforcement
- ☐ Restraining/Protective Order
- ☐ No Trespass order
- ☐ Expected Workplace Conduct Notice/ Acknowledgment
- ☐ Disable computing access
- ☐ FSO notification
- ☐ Collect badge from subject
- ☐ Surveillance requested
- ☐ Document in [insert Company tracking System Name]
- ☐ Other (specify): _____

IX. TMT Members at Initial Meeting:

Discipline	Name	Phone Number
Security & Fire Protection		
Human Resources		
Health Services		
Employee Assistance Program (EAP)		
Law Department		
Corporate Investigations		
Ad Hoc TMT Member (Ethics)		
Ad Hoc TMT Member (EEO)		
Ad Hoc TMT Member (HRI)		
Other Ad Hoc TMT Member (Identify)		
Other Ad Hoc TMT Member (Identify)		
Other Ad Hoc TMT Member (Identify)		
Other Ad Hoc TMT Member (Identify)		

X. Disposition: (Check all that apply):

☐ No further action ☐ Suspension pending investigation ☐ Corrective action ☐ Other (specify) _____

☐ Discharge / termination ☐ Leave of Absence (e.g., Medical, Family, Non-occupational) ☐ Voluntarily Quit

XI. Case Management Updates: (Provide as much details as possible)

Meeting Date:

Attendees (add each name to the table below):

Discipline	Name	Phone Number
Security & Fire Protection		
Human Resources		
Health Services		
Employee Assistance Program (EAP)		

Law Department
Corporate Investigations
Other Ad Hoc TMT Member (Identify)
Other Ad Hoc TMT Member (Identify)
Other Ad Hoc TMT Member (Identify)

Current Threat Level: ☐ Low   ☐ Medium   ☐ High   ☐ Extreme

Brief summary for selected threat level:

Any new action(s) taken:

Category Definitions:
- **Abnormal Behavior:** Causes discomfort to others, deviation from typical patterns and actions, demonstrating emotions of concern
- **Assault:** Any willful attempt or threat to inflict injury upon another person, when coupled with an apparent present ability to do so, or a show of force that creates a reasonable expectation of bodily harm
- **Battery:** Intentionally or recklessly causing offensive physical contact or bodily harm performed against a victim, which is not consented to by the victim. Can be with hands, body, or mechanism
- **Communicated Threat:** An expression of an intention to injure another person. Made verbally, in writing, by gesture, or by electronic means
- **Domestic Violence:** Violence committed by one family member, spouse, former spouse, or household member against another
- **Homicide:** The killing of a human being by another
- **Possession of a Weapon:** The possession of any instrument or device designed, modified, displayed, or used with intent to do bodily harm. This includes functional firearms and other prohibited weapons
- **Stalking:** The act of repeatedly following or harassing another person in circumstances that would cause a reasonable person to fear for his/her safety
- **Suicidal Ideation:** Thoughts of suicide, wishes to die
- **Suicide:** The act or attempt
- **TM Meeting:** When a threat management team meets to work a TM case or for training

No matter which definition you use, what we do know is that metrics, when used correctly, can tell your company's story on what is happening regarding threatening behavior, threats, and acts of violence. This information can then help educate your leadership on the number and types of cases, as well as help design and deploy training and educational resources for your TMTs and your employee population. Metrics are an essential element in your company's program.

Metrics: Ways to Show and Use the Data (Notional Data)

There are many ways to track cases within organizations. Some organizations track cases by region, others by case categories, and some combine the two in order to specifically track issues by location. An example of this is shown in Figure 3.2. Also highlighted are incident rates per number of employees. Rates per number of employee will normalize the data as an organization increases or decreases in employment numbers.

Figure 3.3 shows the top six categories an organization has tracked over a four-year period of time. This can be done in a bar chart format or even a pie chart.

Figure 3.4 shows the total number of cases over a four-year period of time.

What is important to remember is that statistics can help an organization in many ways. Examples of how metric data can be used in your company include:

- Understanding the magnitude of threats, threatening behavior, and acts of violence, by such categories as geographic area and department
- Examining trends in threats, threatening behavior, and acts of violence over time
- Identifying top behavior categories in your company
- Evaluating the effectiveness of your threat management program and new policies and/ or procedures
- Using the information to design training seminars for your TMTs, including specialized threat management WebEx sessions focusing on specific topics, incidents, and trends
- Providing examples for tabletop scenario exercises

Threat Management Cases by Region				*01/01/20XX to 12/31/20XX*		
Categories	**N/W**	**S/W**	**MID & W&E**	**International**	**Enterprise**	**2011**
Abnormal Bahaviour	20	9	8	2	39	40
Assault	40	10	25	1	76	55
Battery	15	10	5		30	5
Communictaed Threats	80	25	45	5	155	135
Domestic Violence	2	2	2		6	4
Homicide					0	0
Possession of Weapon	5	5	5		15	20
Stalking	5	5	6	1	17	15
Suicidal	15	10	5		30	20
Suicide					0	0
Total Cases	**182**	**76**	**101**	**9**	**368**	**294**
Cases per 1,000 Employees	2.04	2.71	2.20	1.13	2.15	1.75
Head Count (as of 12/27/20XX)	89,000	28,000	46,000	8,000	171,000	168,357
Case Trend Against 20XX	↑**38.00%**	↑**16.00%**	↓**13.00%**	**0.00%**	↑**25.00%**	

Figure 3.2 Threat Management Cases by Region and Categories

(a)

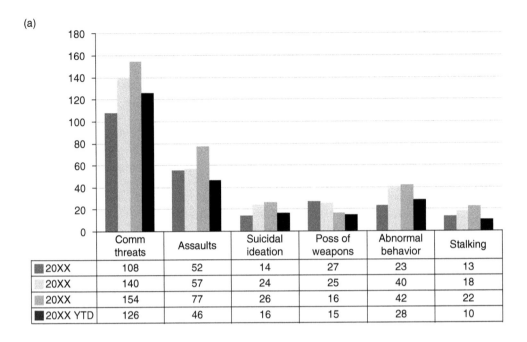

	Comm threats	Assaults	Suicidal ideation	Poss of weapons	Abnormal behavior	Stalking
20XX	108	52	14	27	23	13
20XX	140	57	24	25	40	18
20XX	154	77	26	16	42	22
20XX YTD	126	46	16	15	28	10

(b)

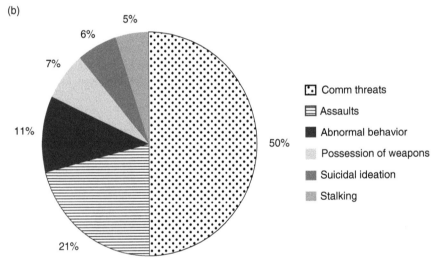

Figure 3.3 Threat Management Cases—Top Six Categories over a Four-Year Period

- Graphically presenting summaries of your company's threat management cases, including trends
- Creating educational resources for management and employees
- Monthly reporting for executive management and key leadership
- Responding to on-demand requests from executives, human resources, security management, company management

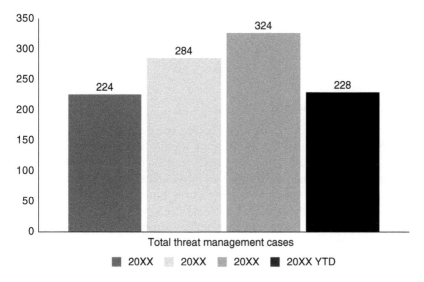

Figure 3.4 Total Number of Threat Management Cases

TIP: *Things to consider when assessing your company's metrics. Focus on the particulars of your cases: "Are there any trends within a specific geographic region, site or building?" Information you can gain from knowing the details of your cases helps you better assess future cases and implement targeted intervention strategies.*

Educating Management and Employees

Taking proper preventive action is essential, and management plays a key role in this process. It is important to educate them on how to identify potential warning signs and people who are exhibiting threatening behavior, threats, and acts of violence. It is also important that they understand their reporting roles and responsibilities.

Acts of violence occur because employees and managers fail to recognize or intervene when there are potential warning signs. When people experience stress for a prolonged period of time and lack coping skills, combined with other indicators such as a history of violence, threatening behavior, threats, and acts of violence may be the consequence. In these cases, the warning signs should be addressed to avert violence. However, an individual may also display one or many potential warning signs and never act out violently. When one or more warning signs are present and the behaviors appear to be increasing in intensity, it might be necessary to intervene. Remember, it is always a good idea to look at the whole picture and not just the situation or moment of concern. Each situation is unique and must be judged on its own facts and circumstances.

Warning signs and contributing factors should be designed into your program. These will help educate management and employees on what to look for and report to security or human resources. Employee need to know how and to whom they can report their concerns and need reassurance that the company is taking their concerns seriously.

> **TIP:** *We recommend creating a threat management guide for managers and a brochure on your program for all employees. Designing a website where employees can go for resources is an excellent idea and allows them to explore privately.*

What Is an Advanced Threat Incident?

An advanced threat incident is defined as "an incident that has the potential for *imminent* serious injury and/or death to an individual(s) at the hand of another whose intent is to harm others." We also see this referred to as an "active threat" or "active shooter." Advanced threat addresses the response to attack by someone with a firearm, an edged weapon, or an instrument that can harm others, and is not limited to only a firearm. The response to any of these attacks should include the same basic elements and options for employees so that they easily understand how to respond to a violent event regardless of the instrument used to carry it out. "Run-Hide-Fight" and "Get Out, Hide Out, Take Out," to name just two, are simple concepts and easily understood and applied by the general public and your employees.

This may not be part of the original deployment of your threat management program, or your company may not want to address this subject initially. However, having a plan prepared may be prudent; sometimes it takes a significant event for your company's executives to embrace launching this portion of the program. As an example, one company's security and human resources directors were proposing to the company's executive leadership team a threat management program and training for managers that include advanced threat incident procedures. The executive leadership responded that "these things don't happen here, we are well educated and we are family." Several months later, a workplace shooting took place at a nearby business and received a great deal of media coverage. Again, the concept of a threat management program and advanced threat incident procedures was proposed, and the executive leadership team agreed it was a good idea, but only made the training recommended and not mandatory.

Then, there are times when some companies will not want to address this at all. No one wants to think about the possibility of someone walking around your workplace injuring or killing your employees and co-workers. An advanced threat incident at your company can have a devastating, long-term impact on your company. This can be a very sensitive subject for companies to talk about. However, you may have employees who have witnessed or been victims of such an incident, or have a family member who was a victim, and it has impacted their lives. When you develop your advanced threat program, like your threat management program, it must be scalable to the resources you have and be actionable.

We have seen companies with on-site armed interdiction teams, companies that rely solely on a law enforcement response, and companies that refuse to talk about or address this topic. There are two phases of training: training for employees and training for the first responders, who could be your security officers, security staff, or law enforcement.

Training your employees on how to react to an advanced threat incident is a proactive approach that will increase their odds of surviving an attack. There are companies that offer off-the-shelf training videos, and these programs are very good and applicable for most businesses and companies. Depending on your company's support or concerns, you may have to work with the supplier of the training video to modify it so that it is acceptable to your human resources and law departments. Some of the videos are very graphic, showing people being shot, and that might not be acceptable to your company. If you use a video for training, you also need to provide the same information in writing, so that if someone declines to watch the video, they still have the opportunity to understand the training and know what their options are for reacting to the advanced threat. Some companies include actual drills as part of their advanced threat training for employees, and while this might work for some, it will not work for others. There are several considerations before conducting a drill. You may have employees who have been victims of or witnesses to an advanced threat incident or have post-traumatic stress disorder (PTSD), and a drill might aggravate their condition. There may also be safety concerns with employees moving quickly throughout your facility, or if someone is not aware that it is a drill and reacts negatively.

Tabletop scenarios should be conducted after viewing the video or being briefed on the training, and this allows employees in a calm and non-stressful situation to think about how they would respond to an advanced threat. They could walk the exit routes to see where each one would take them, and if they had to hide out, which options provide the best protection and which ones do not. This training can help employees think about the "what if" questions and will better prepare them in the case of an advanced threat. As we know from past advanced threat incidents, rarely will law enforcement or security arrive in time to stop the attacker. In this case, your employees need to understand that they are stakeholders in their own safety. When proposing this training to your company's executive leadership, this is a good point to make. Emphasize that you are not trying to frighten your employees; rather, you are giving them the education to react to and possibly survive a violent event.

If your company has offices outside the United States, you will need to design your program to cover both the U.S. and non-U.S. locations. Some countries do not allow or do not address the "Take Out" or "Fight" option due to restrictions or cultural standards. You will need a U.S.-based plan and a non-U.S. plan, or to design your plan so that it is acceptable globally. For the take out or fight option, you might have to word it so that it is left up to the employee how they will respond if they come face to face with the attacker. Let the employee know this is a personal decision on how they will respond to this situation, and let them decide.

Training for first responders and law enforcement outreach is another phase of a successful program. If you have an armed response team on site, how often do they train? Do they train with the law enforcement agencies that would respond to your site? An effective response team should train together once a month to maintain their skills, and train with law enforcement twice a year. Training for a team would include firearms training, searching techniques, and force on force training. The team would need to maintain a level of physical readiness. All of these are perishable skills, and ongoing training is needed to maintain the response capability. The proper training for a response team will require adequate funding and staffing, or the team's ability to effectively respond will be impacted. There are benefits and liabilities to having your own response team, and you will need to evaluate such a capability and determine whether it would be an effective part of your advanced threat program.

Reaching out to the law enforcement agencies that will respond to your company is a critical aspect of your program. Meeting with law enforcement and briefing them on how your company will respond in the event of an advanced threat and how you have trained your employees is essential. You may think that the law enforcement agencies have certain capabilities or preconceived notions about the security or layout of your facility. However, site tours of your facility for the officers, maps, and fact sheets can help them understand where to respond and what hazards there might be at your site. A tabletop exercise on an advanced threat can be very helpful for both you and the agency to understand capabilities, resources, and problematic issues when responding to your site.

> **TIP:** *Reaching out to the commander of the Special Weapons and Tactics (SWAT) or Crisis Response team and asking to meet with them regarding how their agency would respond to your business is one way to establish that relationship. Most SWAT or Crisis Response teams are not contacted by businesses asking to work with them on a response plan for an advanced threat incident. Most teams have a difficult time finding training locations, and offering the team the opportunity to train at your site will benefit both of you.*

Case Example of Working with Law Enforcement: A company had an established relationship with its local law enforcement agency and was dealing with a high-risk termination in a threat management case. The company was concerned that the subject might act out when notified of the termination. Security reached out to the local law enforcement agency and advised them of the pending termination and their concerns with the subject. The agencies had the patrol officers assigned to the area meet with security prior to the termination and were shown where it would occur in case they were called for assistance. The "what if" question was asked, and the proper planning and preparations were implemented, which helped the termination go smoothly.

One tool you can provide to law enforcement when they respond to your site is a "go bag" or a "response kit" that contains maps, access cards, keys, and other items that will help expedite their response and interdiction of an attacker. When meeting with law enforcement, ask them what items would aid their response to an advanced threat incident at your business. Some agencies have told us they will take someone from the security staff with them to unlock doors and help them navigate around a building. This sounds like a good idea, but there are several things to consider before allowing this to happen:

• What is the liability of allowing one of your security employees to respond with the officers?
• Do your security have the proper protective gear or training (i.e., a ballistic vest, physically able), and are they willing to go in harm's way?
• Will your law department allow them to enter with the officers?
• If you have a contract security company providing physical security at your site, you need to know how they train their officers on responding to an advanced threat incident and include them in any planning or tabletop exercises

As with your threat management program, you will need to revisit your advanced threat program after it is launched to ask what is working and what may need to be improved. We would recommend reviewing your program on an annual basis. You might learn that the program is too large and unmanageable, or your resources have changed and you have to amend your approach.

Although it may seem as if a lot of time is being put into planning for an event that may never happen, being unprepared is not worth the gamble, considering the potential impact to your employees, contractors, customers and visitors, property, and business if an act of violence occurs. A genuine commitment to support the safety of all employees, contractors, customers, and visitors, and providing training, open communication, and fair treatment to employees and contractors are all necessary for a safe workplace. You cannot guarantee that violence will never occur; however, early intervention and mitigating strategies will help reduce the risk.

The success of your program depends on all of you working as an integrated team. Quick action, open communication, teaming, and thorough investigations will help mitigate potential incidents and prevent them from escalating into an advanced threat.

4 Principles of Threat Assessment and Management

Just before 8:00 a.m. on September 16, 2013, Aaron Alexis arrived at the Washington Navy Yard. After parking his rented vehicle, he used a valid Common Access Card to enter Building 197. Though he carried a backpack, Alexis was indistinguishable from other contractors and federal employees reporting for work at the Navy Yard that Monday morning. In his backpack, however, Alexis had a Remington 870 shotgun that he had purchased just two days earlier. Alexis had sawn the stock and barrel of the shotgun to shorten its length. Alexis had also carved "Better off this way" and "My ELF weapon" into the stock, which gave an indication of his mental state in the days preceding the shooting.

At 8:16 a.m., less than 15 minutes after entering the building, Alexis began shooting. At 9:25 a.m., law enforcement officers shot Alexis in the head, fatally wounding him. During the intervening 69 minutes, Alexis killed 12 people and wounded several others.

In the following days, the world learned about Aaron Alexis and speculated about what had prompted his horrible rampage.[1]

A common question heard, after one of these horrific mass shootings, is often WHY? Why did the perpetrator come into his or her workplace and kill? What was his or her motivation? Were there warning signs or behaviors of concern that preceded the event, and if those around him or her had known what these signs were, could it have prompted some type of intervention from management, security, or law enforcement to possibly prevent a potentially violent event from happening? Could this same intervention have derailed the individual's path toward violence?

Proactive versus Reactive

Since 9/11, the public has constantly been told by law enforcement and other government officials that citizens have to be alert to unusual circumstances, things out of place, or inappropriate and suspicious behavior when it comes to individuals who might be plotting a terrorist act. "If you see something, say something." We have had to become stakeholders in our own safety and security, as law enforcement cannot be everywhere to identify and prevent these acts. This proactive approach has worked on a number of occasions, as citizens have come forward to report suspicious activity, and some terrorist acts have been averted because of citizen alertness. This same type of approach is what many workplaces have been doing for years, trying to identify the problematic employee and get that individual the help he or she needs to be productive again, or, if need be, in more serious and threatening cases, to mitigate the potential for violence. Reacting to a situation that suddenly occurs limits your options to deal with the situation effectively. Clearly, the best prevention is early intervention, whether it is a potential act of terrorism or an act of workplace violence.

As mentioned in earlier chapters, any prevention strategy has to have in place a program to detect, identify, assess, mitigate, and monitor threats and threatening behavior.[2] A threat management process, utilized by a multi-disciplinary threat management team, will allow the investigation and assessment of potential threats, and, more importantly, deal with the management of a specific threat, by the development of intervention strategies to lower the level of threat. However, before proceeding further, we need to define some important terms.

What Is a Threat?

Webster defines a threat as "an expression of intention to inflict evil, injury or damage, as something that is impending," but who determines whether something is a threat or not? A neutral third party when presented with the investigative facts and circumstances, or is a threat purely in the "eyes of the beholder"? Does the definition have to take on the context of a criminal offense, or can it be described under the rubric of workplace behavior? A threat is defined in the *Workplace Violence Prevention and Intervention* American National Standard, authored by ASIS International and The Society for Human Resource Professionals (SHRM) (2011), as "Any verbal or physical conduct that conveys an intent or is reasonably perceived to convey an intent to cause physical harm or to place someone in fear of physical harm." Others have defined a threat as an expression of intent to do harm that causes a person concern for their own personal safety or the safety of others. Threats can be made verbally, by physical gesture, or in writing and can be conveyed through email, text messaging, social media, or other electronic means. Even if there is no intent of actually carrying it out, if the person reasonably believes that they are in fear for their own safety or the safety of others, then it is a threat. Whatever definition you use, intent and fear for personal safety are a common theme in all of these definitions.

Types of Threat[3]

Threats are made for various reasons: to warn, intimidate, or manipulate a situation or person, to terrorize and frighten, or to force an action and assert power and control. Motivation varies and can range from attention to revenge. Threats can be broken down into four major types: direct, veiled, indirect, and conditional.[4]

Direct Threat

Specific, straightforward, explicit statements of impending harm, such as "I am going to come in and kill everyone in this office!"

Veiled Threat

Sinister innuendo, non-specific statements of impending harm, such as "We would be better off without this manager."

Indirect Threat

Similar to a veiled threat, vague and ambiguous, subtle comments such as "If I wanted to I could kill everyone in this building and get away with it."

Conditional Threat

A statement of harm setting conditions to be met to avert or stop an individual from carrying out the act. "Unless you pay me $5000, I will blow up this building." "If you don't shut down the assembly line tomorrow, I will set off a bomb in the plant."

We have defined what a threat is, and the types of communicated threats; next, we have to define threatening behavior and behaviors of concern.

Threatening Behavior

Sometimes it is an individual's concerning behavior which causes everyone in a work unit to become alarmed and fearful, not a specific threat. This threatening behavior can cause reasonable concern for one's personal safety and/or the safety of others. These behaviors can include, but are not limited to, the following: intimidating or threatening demeanor, bullying, intense uncontrollable rage, intentional physical contact/conduct, angry or argumentative behavior, and unwanted pursuit or stalking.

All threats, whether expressed or communicated by statement or by behavior that is threatening, have to be taken seriously and investigated thoroughly. Once that is done, the analysis of the facts and circumstances surrounding the threat or threatening behavior becomes part of the threat management process. A more formal definition follows.

Threat Management

Threat management is defined as the assessment of and response to threats and threatening behavior. While the focus of threat management is the workplace, a threat made in the workplace toward others outside the workplace, for example, domestic violence (intimate partner) and stalking situations, may also cause the organization to act, including the possible reporting of such a threat to local law enforcement or others as appropriate.

Threat Assessment

"All Threats are **NOT** Created Equal."[5]

It is often difficult to distinguish between a threat that will turn out to be a harmless misunderstanding and a threat that will turn violent. For this reason, all threats, regardless of their perceived severity, should be assessed in a timely manner, and decisions regarding how they are handled must be made quickly. The threat management process has two parts: an evaluation of the threat itself and an evaluation of the person making the threat. These evaluations will help the threat management team (TMT) make an informed judgment as to whether the person making the threat may actually become violent. Mentioned earlier, this assessment also aids in developing the proper intervention strategy or response.

A thorough threat assessment includes analysis of the exact nature and context of the threat, the identified target, the possible motivation of the threat maker, and his or her ability to carry out the threat. The specific questions that have to be answered are: Is the threat credible? Does the threatener have the means, motivation, and wherewithal to carry out the threat?

Other factors impacting the threat assessment include personal background, work history, criminal history, mental health history, and past workplace behavior. Threat assessment refers

---

THREAT ASSESSMENT A TWO – PRONGED APPROACH

In unknown offender cases, the analysis of written, type-written, tape-recorded, and computer-generated threats made against persons, places or things

In known offender cases, the analysis of behaviour exhibited by him/her to assess potential for violence

---

Figure 4.1 Unknown versus Known Offender Assessments

to the actual analysis of a potential threat, whether it is based on a communicated threat being made or problematic behavior observed by co-workers or others. Threat management refers to operational techniques used by the TMT after an initial assessment to respond to a threat of violence.

Identification of Behaviors of Concern

There is no "profile" available to identify future perpetrators of workplace violence. Warning signs, or behaviors of concern if observed by managers or co-workers, can seem ambiguous and are often ignored. In some cases, acts of violence occur because employees do not recognize a potential threat or fail to intervene when they do have concerns about a colleague's behavior. There is no one type of conduct or behavior that can predict whether someone will commit a violent act. However, violence is a process; the behavior in most cases builds over time. It may not be a long period of time, but in some cases it can take years before an act of violence occurs. Generally, after this buildup over time, some type of precipitating event—a reprimand, a poor performance appraisal, a problem with a manager or co-worker—causes an individual to put their plan into action.

In many cases, individuals "leak" behavior. These "clues," looked at independently, may not cause concern; however, when looked at in totality and over time, these behaviors suggest a potential for violence. Much research has been done on "leakage." In an article by Dr. J. Reid Meloy and Mary Ellen O'Toole, leakage is defined as "A communication to a 3rd party of an impending act of targeted violence."[6] This "communication" may be intentional or unintentional. The form of communication varies, but can consist of the following:

- Verbal communication in person or by other electronic means
- Non-verbal gestures
- Cell phone, telephone, voicemails
- Emails/blogs/website postings or use of social media
- Letters/diaries/journals/drawings
- Videos

This "leakage" has occurred preceding a number of mass shooting events, warning individuals known to the perpetrator that something was about to happen.

In addition to this "leakage," sometimes specific behaviors are observed by others which raise the level of concern, such as:

- Communicated threats, threatening behavior, frequent aggressive outbursts, and displays of anger
- A history of threats or violent acts
- Fascination with weapons and/or references to weapons, violent media content, or violent events
- Verbal abuse of co-workers and/or customers, including phone and email harassment
- Unusual or bizarre comments/behavior, especially if they include violent content
- Blaming of others, hypersensitivity to criticism, or holding of grudges
- Sense of entitlement, as if "the rules don't apply"
- Perceived persecution or victimization
- Homicidal/suicidal thoughts or comments
- Depression
- Substance abuse

Not everyone exhibiting these types of behaviors will become violent, but it is important to look at the context and timing of the behavior. In addition, further investigation may suggest mitigating factors which would lower the threat level.

These behaviors are often accompanied by job performance problems, such as inconsistent or decreased productivity, excessive tardiness, and absenteeism, as well as poor relations with co-workers. Problems related to job performance may not indicate an increased propensity for violence, but the examination of these problems could spark additional questions that could reveal behaviors of concern.

Threat Considerations and Stressors

The following threat considerations and stressors may cause an individual prone to violence to act out in the workplace. TMT members should consider the following stressors when conducting a threat assessment:

- Loss or setback: Threat of job loss, marital problems, relationship problems, medical issues
- Mental health issues: Delusional, hallucinating, paranoid, or disoriented behavior
- Behavioral: Erratic, eccentric, hyperactive, or aloof behavior
- Emotional: Agitated or depressed mood
- Substance abuse
- Economic: Inability to pay bills, debts

Precipitating or "Trigger" Events

When combined with the mentioned stressors and behaviors of concern, the following can act as a "trigger" to stimulate a person prone to violence to commit an act of workplace violence. It should be noted that a number of these events are considered a loss to the potential offender, such as:

- Layoff, demotion, termination
- Job reprimand or corrective action
- Negative performance review

Additionally, the perception of the offender is key in how he or she views his/her personal situation and interprets events. This perception is his/her reality, and it is important that TMT members try to look at the issue from the offender's perspective, not to condone actions but to assess risk and anticipate reaction to any intervention strategy that is developed. The following should be considered as part of any threat assessment:

- Perception of harassment
- Perception of consistently not being listened to by others
- Perception of threat to his/her dignity or self worth
- Perceived barrier to object of desire, that is, promotion
- New job, transfer to different location

Assessing the Threat

To determine the level of threat (low, medium, high, or extreme) posed by an individual, an assessment of the threatening behavior should be conducted.

THREAT	INTERVENTION
• Low (minimal threat)	• Interviews & background
• Medium (unclear lethality)	• Additional background & possible law enforcement involvement
• High/Extreme (most serious & least frequent)	• Immediate law enforcement response

Figure 4.2 Levels of Threat and Intervention

Source: O'Toole, Mary Ellen, *The School Shooter: A Threat Assessment Perspective*, Critical Incident Response Group, National Center for the Analysis of Violent Crime, Quantico, VA (1999).

FOUR AREAS OF FOCUS

---

1. Personality of Offender
2. Work Dynamics
3. Family Dynamics
4. Social Factors

Figure 4.3 Threat Evaluation Process

This investigation conducted by TMT personnel will look at all aspects of the life of the individual making the threat in order to evaluate his or her potential for violence. Dr. Mary Ellen O'Toole, when with the FBI's Behavioral Analysis Unit, outlined this approach in the evaluation of threats in school.[7] A similar approach is used in the evaluation of workplace threats.

This evaluation consists of a four-pronged approach:

- The personality of the individual
- The work environment and dynamics and how they impact the individual
- The personal background of the individual
- The individual's social interaction and influences

By talking to others who observed the behavior, an accurate picture of the individual can be developed. Another possible strategy is to interview the subject. This approach must be carefully considered in light of the threat; however, in certain circumstances such an interview could provide valuable insight into the subject's thinking and might prove to be a vehicle to change his or her behavior. These interview strategies should be discussed with fellow TMT members as part of an overall investigative/intervention strategy.

Personality

Personality shapes how we view the world and how we interact with others. It is who we are. Individual personality traits can be observed when that same person has to cope with disappointment, loss, or failure. Some questions to consider as part of the assessment process:

- Does he/she bounce back when encountering a setback or personal difficulty?
- How does he/she cope with disappointment?
- Does he/she desire to be in control?
- Can the individual accept responsibility for his/her actions?

- Is there a lack of empathy?
- Is there a perception that he/she has been wronged in some way?
- How does he/she relate to others?

Work Dynamics

This includes interaction with co-workers, problems with specific managers or management in general, excess concern about job responsibilities, concern about layoffs or downsizing, a recent reprimand or poor performance review, and perception of unfair treatment. Other issues include the nature of the work environment, the tolerance of harassment or bullying, and the effectiveness of management.

Personal Issues

Personal issues include any family problems, including divorce, child custody issues, a death in the family, or other personal loss. Financial issues, such as high personal debt, bankruptcy, and high medical bills, should also be considered. Other possible factors include a known history of substance abuse, mental illness, or depression.

Interests or Societal or Social Influences

Information that can assist in understanding an individual's background can come from a variety of sources. Personnel records are a good resource, including educational history, employment history, performance appraisals, disciplinary history, and any special skills, such as military or police training. Interviews with former managers and co-workers and records from various sources, including medical, credit, police, and military records, should all be sought. The following characteristics may also be of interest when evaluating a potential threat:

- Does the individual show an interest in violence through movies, video games, books, magazines, or social media?
- Is there a preoccupation with violent themes or revenge?
- Does the individual have a fascination with and/or recent acquisition of weapons?
- Does he/she possess any weapons?
- Has he/she communicated any thoughts or plans for violence?
- Has he/she identified a target?

Evaluation of the Threat

Once information is gathered, it is analyzed to determine the level of risk posed by an individual for acting out violently in the workplace. The first task is to evaluate all behaviors of concern which might elevate the risk of a violent incident. The analysis should then take into consideration any mitigating factors, such as a strong family support system, strong ties to a community, or a lack of previous problems or behaviors.

While TMT members have had specific training to aid them in determining the risk level or level of threat posed by an individual to others or to the organization, there may be a time when an outside consultant, who has the requisite education, background, and experience in dealing with violence and its potential, is brought in by the team to assist and/or provide a more formal threat assessment and assist in the management of a case. These individuals should be vetted by the team and put in place as soon as necessary.

Considerations for Investigation, Intervention, and Case Management

Extreme threats, such as an active shooter, require an immediate law enforcement response. High-level threats could also require an immediate response from law enforcement, depending on case circumstances. With low- to medium-level threats, the use of law enforcement may be an option. In these situations, intervention strategies have to be developed to lower the level of threat. Intervention involves developing a plan that convinces the individual not to use violence to solve employment-related problems. Intervention strategies vary from case to case, as each situation is different; there is no one size fits all strategy. It is a process that must be carried out in consultation with other members of the TMT.

Intervention strategies should be viewed on a continuum. They include the monitoring of a situation in an unobtrusive way, providing coaching or training to the employee, providing psychological counseling to the employee, transferring the employee, restructuring the position, taking disciplinary action, or suspending or terminating the individual's employment. Other possibilities might include offering a severance package or providing outplacement services and employment counselors.

Employees should be treated with dignity and respect whenever possible. This will contribute to a corporate environment of fairness and professionalism and will also lower the potential for violence: an employee who believes that he or she has been treated fairly will be less likely to act violently.

We have explained the threat management process, defined terms, and identified behaviors of concern and what is needed by TMTs to conduct a threat assessment; let's see how that may apply to the case example we began this chapter with.

Limitations of Threat Assessment

There are limitations to determining level of risk. A threat assessment made by the TMT or qualified professional is an opinion, based upon available facts and circumstances as determined by investigation. It can change as additional information is developed or circumstances change. The management of threats is a dynamic process.

As we have seen, individuals make threats for a variety of reasons; sometimes those reasons are only known to the threatener. Many make threats yet do not pose a threat; some who make threats or display threatening behavior may pose a threat; and others pose a threat without making threats or displaying any concerning behavior at all, and commit a violent act. Through the threat management process, the TMT must determine those who pose an actual risk to an organization.

Washington Navy Yard Shooting

Aaron Alexis was born on May 9, 1979, in Queens, New York. He attended high school in the Bronx, and in May 2007, Alexis joined the Navy and served as an aviation electrician before being honorably discharged in January 2011. He was then transferred to reserve status.

Both prior to and following his military service, Alexis lived a rather transient life that included several moves around the country and contract employment overseas. There were periods of unemployment, temporary work as a waiter, and studies at technical schools.

In late 2012, The Experts, Inc., employed him to provide IT support for the Navy in Japan, which was followed by similar work at installations in various locations in the United States.

Before arriving in Washington, DC, Alexis had three encounters with law enforcement:

- 2004—Seattle, Washington—Alexis shot out tires of a vehicle following an angry confrontation with a construction worker in the neighborhood where he was living at the time. Alexis did not recall his actions due to black-outs caused by extreme anger. He allegedly suffered from PTSD as a result of assisting after the 9/11 attacks
- 2008—Arrested for disorderly conduct in DeKalb County, Georgia
- 2010—Ft. Worth, Texas—Discharged a firearm into the ceiling of the apartment he was living in at the time, an accidental discharge while he was cleaning the weapon

Despite previous incidents, no documented reports of any issues were reported by co-workers or supervisors working with Alexis.

Since coming to Washington, DC, Alexis allegedly sought treatment at two different VA hospitals for insomnia, but denied having any depressive episodes or other psychological issues. Alexis later told police in Rhode Island that he believed voices were harassing him and that the government was doing a microwave project on him. This incident was allegedly reported to the Navy.

Two days prior to the shooting, Alexis went to a firearms dealer in Virginia with the intent of purchasing an AR-15 rifle, but was refused because he was not a Virginia resident. He purchased a Remington model 870 pump shotgun instead. He later purchased a hacksaw to cut down the barrel and the stock. He also inscribed several messages on the weapon: "Better off this way," "My ELF weapon," and "Not what you say." It was that weapon and the weapon obtained from a security guard after killing him that he used to attack workers at the Washington Navy Yard.

While hindsight is 20/20, based upon what we know now, is it possible that this incident could have been prevented? Were there opportunities missed that, if dealt with at an earlier stage, might have at least interrupted his path toward violence? If information about previous behavior had been made known to the Navy or to the contractor he was employed by, could some type of intervention have taken place to deal with his alleged mental health issues? If these unusual and strange behaviors had been known, and if there had been a threat management process in place as described (the Navy does have access to trained individuals at the Naval Criminal Investigative Service (NCIS) and the FBI), could some type of intervention strategy have been developed so that his strange behavior would be dealt with, and perhaps he would have gotten the mental health treatment that he apparently needed? These are questions that will be dealt with in any civil legal proceedings that often come after these horrific events.

We have seen similar questions asked after the mass shootings perpetrated by James Holmes in the movie theater in Aurora, Colorado, by Adam Lanza at the elementary school in Newtown, Connecticut, and by Dylan Roof, who killed nine church members at AME church in Charleston, South Carolina.

While no one can predict with certainty what another individual will do, clearly we know that no one "snaps"; in most cases there are warning signs, behaviors of concern, previous threats, and a history of violence. The perpetration of violence is an evolutionary process; it develops over time. Our collective goal is to put processes in place to identify problematic individuals early before behavior escalates and might ultimately erupt into a horrific violent event, which of late has seemed to be all too common.

Notes

1. Committee on Oversight and Government Reform, U.S. House of Representatives, Staff Report, *Slipping through the Cracks: How the D.C. Navy Yard Shooting Exposes Flaws in the Federal Security Clearance Process*, Washington, DC (2014).

2. Rugala, E.A., Fitzgerald, J.R., Workplace violence: From threat to intervention, *Clinics in Occupational and Environmental Medicine*, 775–789 (2003).

3. Ibid.

4. O'Toole, Mary Ellen, *The School Shooter: A Threat Assessment Perspective*, Critical Incident Response Group, National Center for the Analysis of Violent Crime, Quantico, VA (1999).

5. Ibid.

6. Meloy, J. Reid, O'Toole, Mary Ellen, The concept of leakage in threat assessment, *Behavioral Science and the Law*, 513–527 (2011).

7. Ibid., *supra* note 4.

5 Legal Considerations in the Management of Threats

Michael A. Crane, Esq. and Matthew W. Doherty
Senior Vice Presidents of the Threat Violence Risk Management Practice at Hillard Heintze

With assistance and research by Heather Stallings, J.D. Candidate 2018, DePaul University School of Law; Mary Macleod, J.D. Candidate 2018, Loyola University Chicago School of Law; and Elena Sakelaris, J.D. Candidate 2018, Loyola University Chicago School of Law

In previous chapters we discussed the role of the multi-disciplinary threat management team in the controlling of threats and threatening behavior. This team consists of representatives from security, human resources, legal, occupational health, employee assistance, and other ad hoc members as needed—such as union representatives and management personnel. This team is tasked with the assessment of threats and threatening behavior, to assign a level of risk, and to determine strategies to mitigate the potential threat. An important member of this team is legal counsel.

Whether in-house or external to the organization, legal counsel plays a pivotal role by ensuring that the organization "has met legal requirements related to the prevention of workplace violence, as well as assuring that the organization has considered and properly navigated the myriad of legal issues that arise during incident management."[1] This process can roughly be broken down into three components: pre-incident, during an incident, and post-incident.

Pre-Incident

This process can first be evaluated by looking at the different laws that regulate this field from a federal, state, and common law perspective, so that the employer can develop a plan that is a legal response to workplace violence.

1. The Constitution

The Constitution restricts what an employer may do to prevent workplace violence. Employee speech is generally protected unless it is considered to be a "true threat."[2] True threats are not protected as free speech under the First Amendment. A "true threat" is defined as a serious expression of an intent to harm as distinguished from hyperbole, jest, or other innocuous talk or political expressions. Additionally, true threats are "speech that a reasonable person would foresee as a serious expression of intent to harm or assault."[3] Under this analysis, an employer may take action against the person who made the threat only when a statement is considered to be a true threat. However, this action will be limited by several federal, state, and common laws set forth in this chapter.

2. *Federal Law*

Federal law sets the floor for what an employer must provide for its employees in terms of safety. The Department of Labor (DOL) sets certain standards, which include breaks and meal times, work hours, wages, and anti-discrimination regulations. Additionally, the DOL created the Occupational Health and Safety Act of 1970[4] (OSHA).

OSHA's "General Duty" clause states that employers have the general duty under the Act to furnish each employee with "a place of employment that is free from recognized hazards that are causing or are likely to cause death or serious physical harm"[5] and to "comply with occupational safety and health standards promulgated under this Act."[6] Like the constitutional requirement, a threat of violence under OSHA must also be foreseeably harmful to a reasonable person. The "General Duty" clause is often applied as a catch-all category, which courts have applied to situations where the Act is silent. The "General Duty" clause has been applied to workplace violence when such violence has reached the point of being a foreseeable or recognized hazard.[7] In *National Realty and Construction Company, Inc. v. OSHRC*, the court held that Congress did not intend unpreventable hazards; Congress only requires the elimination of "recognized" hazards.[8] However, in application, the states tend to disagree on what a "recognized" hazard is; therefore, there is no uniform application of OSHA's general duty clause.

Moreover, in *Franklin v. The Monadnock Co.*,[9] an employee alleged that a co-worker threatened to have him and three of his colleagues killed. The employee then alleged that the employer did nothing in response to the employee's complaint about the threats, and that the co-worker then assaulted him. The employee then reported the incident to law enforcement. The reporting employee was subsequently terminated from the company as a result of these complaints. The Second District stated that the company had the duty to keep employees safe from harm, including that employers must take reasonable steps to address credible threats of violence in the workplace. The employee who reported the threat was able to make a wrongful termination claim against the employer for not upholding its duty.

There are other major federal laws in this field; however, workplace regulations are typically left to the states for proactive regulation. This chapter will go into more depth regarding the applicable federal laws in the "during" and "post"-incident management sections.

3. *State Law*

State laws vary widely in what they require of employers in terms of workplace violence prevention and pre-incident management. OSHA allows states to either adopt its regulations entirely or set their own standards, which must be equally exacting as OSHA's. Many states have adopted OSHA in its entirety; however, this section examines the range of regulations and statutes that states have implemented.[10]

An important and developing issue in state law interpretation of OSHA is the "parking-lot law." These laws prohibit employers from preventing their employees from storing legally possessed firearms in the employee's legally parked vehicle in the employer's parking lot. Florida and Oklahoma have both stated that OSHA does not preempt such state legislation because businesses have no duty under the Federal Act to ban guns from their workplaces. Additionally, these states have concluded that since OSHA does not explicitly mention firearms,[11] OSHA cannot preempt what it does not speak on.[12] Additionally, the drafters of OSHA were aware of any controversy surrounding firearms in the workplace and consciously decided not to adopt such a standard.[13] The Oklahoma parking-lot law absolves employers from any liability following from a lawfully stored firearm on their property and holds employers criminally liable for prohibiting employees from storing firearms in company vehicles on company property.[14]

There are now 22 states with similar statutes to those of Florida and Oklahoma.[15] California has taken the opposite stance in its state law workplace violence regime. California requires all employers to establish an Injury and Illness Prevention (IIP) Program. This places a legal obligation on employers to provide and maintain a safe and healthful workplace for employees, which may be extended to apply to violence.[16] California's Department of Occupational Safety and Health Standards (DOSH) is similarly regulatory as its federal counterpart; it specifically addresses workplace violence and how it may be handled.[17] However, this regulation does suggest an individualized approach to the prevention of violence, such as "panic buttons" in hospitals and "hand held alarms" for site workers.[18]

Washington State specifically encourages employers to take steps to eliminate easy access to potential weapons and to provide access to communication systems for alerting and reporting. This is one of the only states to address weapons directly as opposed to leaving the determination up to a type of "catch-all" clause. Additionally, the Washington regulation identifies four different types of workplace violence, which intends to put employers on notice of the specific risks unique to each type. Additionally, late-night retail employers are required to implement detailed employee training programs and specified design features.[19]

Furthermore, worker compensation models vary state-by-state and play a factor in workplace violence situations. States like California and Pennsylvania seek to deter workplace violence by barring recovery of benefits when the employee violates the company's policy and the violent action constitutes willful misconduct. In the Pennsylvania case *Johns v. Unemployment Comp. Bd. of Review*, the former employee threatened another co-worker, which was relayed to management. The employee was then terminated following an investigation.[20] Initially, the employee received state unemployment compensation; however, upon appeal to a referee and finding of willful misconduct on the part of the employee, compensation was terminated. The *Johns* court determined that threatening a co-worker falls into the category of willful misconduct, and if the employer can establish the existence of the rule, the reasonableness of the rule, and the claimant's knowledge of the rule, and its violation resulted in an appropriate denial of his unemployment compensation benefits, then denial is appropriate. It is important to note that the court stressed the employer's explicit policy against such threatening behavior, and that violation of that policy gave rise to the willful conduct. Without implementing the policy, even though it was not legally required to do so, the employer would not have won the appeal.

4. Common Law and Classic Tort Claims

Some companies choose the economic approach of not committing to a workplace violence policy or safety regime because the odds of an incident occurring are low and it is therefore reasonable for an employer to deal with violence retroactively. However, the following common law principles rest on the idea of foreseeability. Therefore, since it has been established that workplace violence is a foreseeable and preventable hazard, the question becomes to what extent an employer should take action to absolve itself from liability to its employees, customers, clients, and patients.

Courts are split on whether a violation of OSHA is indicative of negligence.[21] Generally, there is no duty to warn or protect others absent a special relationship.[22] In some working environments that relationship exists; some examples are employees, contractors, suppliers, tenants, students, and invited guests. When there is a special relationship established, the expectation for the defendant employer to warn or protect increases in proportion to the increased apparent likelihood and gravity of possible harm. This is where a workplace violence policy and reporting system becomes essential. Risk assessment does not absolve the employer of liability, but it can help determine how the employer may be liable and how the employer can protect and warn. This is also very important when workplace violence may present a greater risk to the client or customer rather than to the employee. For example, a rider of the Chicago Transit Authority "L" Trains is at a greater risk of violence than the employee, but the employer may be held liable to both parties if there was a foreseeable and preventable risk.

OSHA and its state counterparts generally extend to the protection of employees. For non-employees and unprotected employees to make a claim that the employer was not performing its duty of care, there are several common law causes of action. Typically these are vicarious liability, negligent hiring, negligent retention, negligent supervision, and the duty to investigate dangerous situations and inadequate security, which will be discussed later in the post-incident section of this chapter.

During an Incident

During an incident, legal counsel, working within the framework of the multi-disciplinary threat management team, might advise on some of the following issues: An Employee's Right to Privacy; The Americans with Disabilities Act (ADA); Wrongful Termination and Due Process; Rights under a Collective Bargaining Agreement; Discrimination; and a Hostile Work Environment.

1. An Employee's Right to Privacy

Investigations of violence or threats by a threat management team will often raise privacy issues. A team will commonly need to search computers, desks, and lockers for evidence of threats or for weapons. Moreover, a team may need to conduct a psychological evaluation and collect an employee's personal information in order to make a violence risk assessment. Legal counsel can help the organization define the actions that are permissible and those that may violate an employee's privacy rights.

An employee's right to privacy differs between public and private institutions. The Constitution of the United States protects people's right to privacy under the Fourth Amendment.[23] There are multiple privacy interests for organizations to address with their legal counsel in the public sphere. One is the employee's right to confidentiality.[24] A court, when deciding this issue, will balance the government's interest in attaining this information against an "individual's privacy interest."[25] Courts use the "reasonable expectation of privacy" test to determine whether the information being sought can be seized by the employer. The amount of leeway that is granted by the courts depends on what type of work the employee does and what information they have access to on a daily basis. For example, in *National Treasury Employees Union v. U.S. Department of Treasury*, the court stated that because the employees were public trust employees at the Internal Revenue Service (IRS) who had "access to … financial and other personal and confidential information," it was important for the IRS to determine an employee's chances of misconduct or misfeasance.[26] Therefore, these employees had a diminished reasonable expectation of privacy when asked about their drug and alcohol use in the past.[27] The balancing test here is between the government's interest to know whether individuals with access to sensitive information may have drug and alcohol weaknesses and the employee's desire to keep this information private. In this case, the court emphasized that the outcome would have been different if the IRS publicly disclosed this information.[28]

Moreover, in the context of search, the Court stated that the Fourth Amendment probable cause standard does not apply in the workplace.[29] Therefore, even if an employee has a reasonable expectation of privacy, the search will be allowed if it is justified at its inception and reasonable in scope.[30]

In contrast, private sector employees have no concrete protections under federal law. However, courts will often look to common law and use a similar "reasonable expectation of privacy" test for private sector employees.[31]

For example, in *K-Mart Corp. Store No. 7441 v. Trotti*, the court found that an employee who uses her own lock on a company locker used to store personal items has a reasonable expectation of privacy.[32] Moreover, in *Doe v. Kohn Nast & Graf, P.C.*, the court ruled that an employee has a reasonable expectation of privacy regarding mail marked personal that is delivered to his workplace.[33] However, in *Acosta v. Scott Labor LLC*, the court held that employees did not have a reasonable expectation of privacy in the shared offices of their workplace; therefore there was no violation when employees were videotaped without their consent.[34]

Additionally, businesses usually are allowed by federal and state law to "monitor electronic communications [due to] the business use exception, the system provider exception, and the consent exception."[35] An employer can diminish the possibility of violations by "clarify[ing] its intent for a court by documenting *specific* contract provisions about how and what records are to be kept, and by informing employees about the relevant provisions of that contract."[36]

Any of the aforementioned rights to privacy issues can also be solved by explicit consent. Both public and private employees can waive their right to privacy and consent to any search.

2. The Americans with Disabilities Act (ADA) and Americans with Disabilities Act Amended (ADAA)

Investigations of violence or threats by a threat management team will often also raise ADA issues. An employee who is displaying threatening or suspicious behavior may be suffering from a mental illness or psychological disability. If so, these employees are entitled to rights under the ADA and related state law. Legal counsel can help the organization comply with these rights in situations that involve a need to terminate, discipline, or otherwise manage an employee whose threatening or disturbing behavior may stem from mental or physical impairment.

The ADA applies to any employer with 15 or more employees.[37] These employers must provide a disabled individual with an equal opportunity to the "full range of employment-related opportunities available to others."[38] Under the ADA, someone is considered "disabled if: (1) The person is substantially impaired with respect to a major life activity; (2) The person has a record of such an impairment; or (3) The person is regarded as having such an impairment."[39] Moreover, any person who has an association with an individual who is disabled, such as a relative or any person who suffered retaliation for helping a disabled person assert their rights under the ADA, is protected.[40] Employers must not violate the ADA when terminating an employee for threats or potential instances of workplace violence, and must have adequate grounds for dismissal that make it clear that the termination was not due to a protected disability.

Unlike the Fourth Amendment "right to privacy" protections, which apply to the public sector but not the private sector, the ADA applies to both the public and private sectors. Private sector organizations are expected to comply even if their state of incorporation is not regulated by the ADA.[41] Moreover, the legislative intent behind the ADA "indicate[s] that Congress targeted the ADA at employment discrimination in the private sector."[42]

3. Wrongful Termination and Due Process

Investigations of violence or threats by a threat management team will often also raise issues relating to an employee's alleged wrongful termination. For example, an employer who terminates an employee following a reported threat or violent act, but who has failed to properly investigate or failed to establish sufficient grounds, may be faced with claims of wrongful termination. Legal counsel can help guide an internal investigation and help to ensure full compliance with an employee's rights as shaped by constitutional and contractual principles affecting both private and public sector employers.

A public sector employee does have protections under procedural due process from wrongful termination. There is a two-pronged test under the Fourteenth Amendment: "(1) Did the individual possess a protected interest to which due process protection was applicable? (2) Was the individual afforded an appropriate level of process?"[43] The Fourteenth Amendment protects against the deprivation of life, liberty, or property without due process of law.[44]

Furthermore, many states have statutes allowing employees to bring civil action against their employer for wrongful termination. Moreover, while procedural due process does not strictly apply to employment, an employee should receive notice and be aware of what his or her employer is investigating.[45] Additionally, the employee should see the allegations being levied against him or her so he or she has an opportunity to rebut them.[46]

Lastly, it is important to consider whether the state the organization is located in is an at-will employment state, because this type of employment allows an employee/employer relationship to be terminated for any reason or no reason.

4. Rights under a Collective Bargaining Agreement

Moreover, an employer who acts too swiftly to terminate a worker who has engaged in threatening or violent behavior, or who fails to follow negotiated investigative or disciplinary procedures, may be challenged by a union for violating the terms of a collective bargaining agreement. Legal counsel can help ensure an organization's compliance with the terms of any relevant labor agreement.

The National Labor Relations Act[47] (NLRA) guarantees the right for employers and employees to engage in a collective bargaining agreement. A collective bargaining agreement is a contract between an employer and a union representing a group of employees. The agreement is applicable to the terms of the employment and likely will include a clause regarding wrongful termination or reasons an employee can be terminated. If an employer violates a collective bargaining agreement, it can be sued by the union on behalf of the employee.

5. Discrimination

Furthermore, an employer must carry out workplace violence prevention, intervention, and response policies fairly and uniformly, lest it be accused of applying these policies in a discriminatory fashion. Oversight by legal counsel can contribute to a consistent application of the employer's policies and procedures or practices related to violence prevention, intervention, and response.

In the Civil Rights Act of 1964, Title VII, which applies to both public and private sector employees, protects against discrimination in the workplace. The employee can sue for damages if he or she was discriminated against by "race, color, religion, sex, or national origin within the meaning of section 703 of the Civil Rights Act of 1964."[48] Furthermore, age and disability have been added in later amendments.[49] The addition of these protected classes of persons is relevant because, as with the ADA, an employer must show in cases of wrongful termination that the termination was not motivated by discrimination against one of the protected classes.

6. Hostile Work Environment

Public and private organizations must also respect their employees' right not to work in a hostile work environment. Commonly, workplace violence and threats of violence are aimed at specific groups (e.g. gender, race, ethnicity, religion, and so forth), creating situations of abuse and hostility. The legal team should take steps to prevent this type of environment from developing during an incident of workplace violence.

To establish a hostile work environment, an employee must prove in his or her complaint that the conduct was unwelcome, offensive, sexual (or insulting to another protected class), or directed at the employee because of sex (or other protected class).[50] The conduct also must be serious and so unescapable that it substantially alters the employee's ability to work.[51] The workplace must be considered "an abusive working environment."[52] Moreover, the employer must know or should have known that the in-question conduct was occurring and that it failed to stop the conduct.[53]

In certain circumstances, such as stalking situations, legal counsel may lead in efforts to obtain a corporate restraining order or engage in other legal process.

Post-Incident

The effects of workplace violence extend beyond the incident. Especially for an employer, an incident of workplace violence can result in lawsuits based on various aspects of liability. Employers can be sued by a victim of workplace violence under the theory of negligent hiring, negligent retention, and negligent supervision. Employers can also face liability for failing to take the necessary steps to prevent an instance of workplace violence when they have effective knowledge that an incident could occur, should have known an incident could have occurred, or failed to provide the appropriate work environment required under OSHA. Unfortunately for employers, workplace violence is so volatile that it is difficult to predict what steps will be necessary to prevent or mitigate an incident, and it is also difficult to preemptively act when federal and state law is so inconsistent and incomplete on the issue of workplace violence and the duty employers possess.

1. The Exclusivity Rule and Recovery

Previously, under the exclusivity rule, an employee could only recover from the employer if the incident occurred during the scope of employment.[54] This scheme made it extremely difficult for employees to recover damages from the employer due to the fact that if the injury occurred outside the scope of employment, the employer would not be held liable. Under the exclusivity rule, the "scope of employment" generally was construed very narrowly, which effectively prevented valuable recovery.

Many states sought to find a way to protect employees from this limited recovery by passing workers' compensation statutes; however, these statutes still fall short because they effectively bar employees from suing their employer for tort damages—including negligent hiring, retention, and supervision.[55] Courts have attempted to read an exception into workers' compensation statutes through the intentional tort theory, in which the employer must have acted intentionally or deliberately to injure an employee.[56] This requires actual knowledge of a condition that poses a threat of harm to an employee, and will be viewed as deliberate or intentional only when the employer allows the condition to continue.[57] A failure to take necessary steps when faced with known or suspected dangers may also be considered an intentional action on the part of the employer. Courts have been known to go both ways in regard to intentional tort theory for employers, and therefore this unpredictability encourages employers to settle claims to avoid an overly sympathetic jury.

2. Common Law Liability

Under common law, employer liability stems from the master–servant relationship that comes from agency law. Restatement of Agency Law §219(1) states: "a master is subject to liability for the torts of his servants committed while acting in the scope of their employment."[58] Courts have favored interpreting the phrase "scope of employment" fairly broadly. The master-employer also owes a duty to protect the servant-employee from harm, and if an employee is injured within the scope of his or her employment, the employer will be liable for breaching its duty of care.

The scope of employment includes the conduct one is employed to perform and occurs substantially within the authorized time and space limits of employment.[59] An employer can be directly liable to an employee for acting wrongfully toward him or her; an employer can assume responsibility for harm by ratifying the wrongful behavior or by failing to fulfill the employer's obligation to protect.[60] A plaintiff must establish all the elements of common law negligence—duty, breach, causation, and harm—to hold the employer liable under a negligence theory.[61]

3. Negligent Hiring

The first theory under which an employer can be held liable in instances of workplace violence is negligent hiring. An employer negligently hires if ordinary care is not exercised during the hiring process and through the hiring practices.[62] An injured employee can assert a claim for negligent hiring when the employer failed to take minimum steps to ensure new employees or prospective employees do not pose a threat to the existing employees. A court can find an employer liable for negligent hiring if the employer failed to have a screening process for potential employees, did not conduct sufficient background checks on prospective employees, or did not check the references of an applicant. If the employer could have discovered a potential red flag, that is, a propensity toward violence or criminal records, through a reasonably diligent search, but failed to do so, the court could find the employer liable for negligent hiring.

To prevail under a negligent hiring claim, the plaintiff must establish that: (1) an employment relationship exists; (2) the employee is incompetent; (3) the employer had actual or constructive knowledge of the incompetence; (4) the employer's act or omission caused the plaintiff's injuries; (5) the negligent hiring was the proximate cause of the plaintiff's injuries; and (6) the actual damage or harm resulted from the tortious act.[63] Generally, most claims for negligent hiring rest on the issue of foreseeability—was it foreseeable at the time employment was offered that the individual potentially could pose a threat to the workplace? If a court determines that yes, it was foreseeable, the employer can face liability for failing to exercise due care in conducting a reasonable investigation before hiring the individual.

4. Negligent Supervision and Retention

Next, employers can face liability for negligent supervision. Unlike negligent hiring, in cases of negligent supervision, the employer was not previously aware of the potential risk until after the employee was hired. Just as in a negligent hiring suit, the plaintiff's injury must have been foreseeable for liability to be attached to the employer. A negligent hiring claim also requires that the employer failed to properly train or supervise the employee.[64] In *Faragher v. City of Boca Raton*, the Supreme Court held that an employer could be liable for the sexual harassment committed by one of the supervisors against one of their subordinates because the city did not exercise reasonable care to ensure the work environment was free of foreseeable harms.[65] The Court went on to say that it is reasonable to "hold an employer vicariously liable for some tortious conduct of a supervisor made possible by abuse of his supervisory authority, and that the aided-by-agency-relationship principle found in the restatement provides an appropriate starting point for determining liability."[66] The supervisor was in a position to abuse his power over the subordinates through sexual harassment, and the employer was in a position to foresee this type of potential harm.

However, the Court said that an employer does reserve a two-part defense to such claims of liability. First, the defense can argue that "the employer exercised reasonable care to prevent and correct promptly any sexually harassing behavior," and second, "the plaintiff employee unreasonably failed to take advantage of any preventive or corrective opportunities provided by the employer or to avoid harm otherwise."[67] The employer must establish both elements to avoid liability. In this case, the employer was found liable for failing to properly supervise its employees and failing to respond to or investigate claims made by the plaintiff regarding the harassment.

This case stands to show that the best way for an employer to protect itself from a negligent retention suit would be through an immediate response with appropriate precautions against further harm once the employer is aware of an employee's violent or harassing tendencies. This case further illustrates the importance of an employer's duty in providing a safe work environment. Failure to ensure the workplace is and remains threat-free could open the employer to further issues of negligent retention and supervision.

Another example of an employer being held liable for the wrongdoings of employees is found in *Doe v. XYC Corp*. In this case, the court held that "an employer who is on notice that one of its employees is using a workplace computer to access pornography, possibly child pornography, has a duty to investigate the employee's activities and to take prompt and effective action to stop the unauthorized activity, lest it result in harm to innocent third-parties."[68] The court held that the employer had the control to monitor an employee's activities at the office specifically in regard to internet usage, that the employer was on notice through the supervisor and management personnel that the employee was viewing pornographic materials on the work computer, and that the employer owed the plaintiff a duty of care under the basic fairness of public policy.[69] Furthermore, the plaintiff presented evidence that had the employer conducted a minimal investigation it would have discovered the employee's illegal activities, and therefore it had a duty to report those activities to the authorities and take internal action to stop the viewing of child pornography and circulation of photos of the employee's stepdaughter. This case clearly demonstrates that an employee can be held liable for failing to take the necessary action or conducting the minimal level of investigation to ensure employees are not engaging in harmful or illegal conduct.

5. Problems with Avoiding Liability

However, it is not so cut and dried for employers to avoid liability. The first instinct many people have is to immediately fire an employee who shows a propensity toward violence or represents a potential threat to the workplace. This method is problematic for reasons beyond the basic fact that often instances of workplace violence are committed by disgruntled former employees. Employers must consider the rights of employees under Title VII, non-discrimination rights, the Family and Medical Leave Act (FMLA),[70] and the

Americans with Disabilities Act (ADA), as mentioned previously. Each of these provides an employee with protection against wrongful termination. For example, under the FMLA, an employer may not terminate an employee who has opted to exercise his or her right to take temporary leave in order to address an issue of mental health. Furthermore, under the FMLA, if an employer dismisses an employee while they are utilizing their FMLA rights, the employer must show that termination was not related to the medical leave, and in instances of workplace violence an affected employee may exercise their rights under FMLA to tend to the injury.

Avoiding negligent hiring claims can be extremely difficult, because an employer cannot discriminate against an individual with a qualified disability, and the ADA places severe limitations on an employer from inquiring too intensely into an individual's disability.[71] The methods for screening a potentially violent employee can be legally excessive, and there is a lack of uniform guidelines or requirements regarding prescreening.[72] Furthermore, Title VII of the Civil Rights Act of 1964 precludes an employer from asking a potential employee about his or her arrest record, and a record of an arrest does not equate to guilt.[73] Because of the vast protections granted to employees, it is difficult for employers to preemptively prevent workplace violence from occurring.

6. OSHA

Employers can look to OSHA for guidance in preventing or mitigating workplace violence instances. Though OSHA provides general guidelines for employers, as previously discussed at the beginning of this chapter, the important thing to remember is that OSHA is not binding law; courts, along with the Secretary of Labor, reserve the right to determine whether there have been violations of the standards and what the penalty for those violations should be.[74] Employers do have an obligation to provide security to employees and to control the action of employees under the employer–employee relationship, and under this duty courts assign liability to employers for failing to furnish a safe workplace and failing to take action when on notice in regard to a potential harm.

7. Temporary Restraining Orders (TROs)

Another option for employers is to obtain a TRO in response to the threat of workplace violence. TROs provide employers with increased protection for the company and employees and reduce potential employer liability by existing as an intermediate measure taken to mitigate a potential incident.[75] A TRO functions similarly to a TPO (temporary protective order), which would be issued in cases of domestic violence. It is faster acting than other legal measures and allows the employer to immediately respond to potential threats by temporarily restricting access by the threatening individual.[76] This method allows an employer to prevent a potential instance by intervening before the instance has occurred. While the TRO is a logical option for an employer to mitigate potential liability and harm, not all states have implemented an option for an employer to obtain a TRO.

Final Thoughts

As this chapter has illustrated, while employers have access to legal resources to prevent and protect against instances of workplace violence, there are still many legal hurdles employers must overcome. First, employers are prevented from outright refusing to hire or fire a potentially dangerous individual if they qualify as one of the protected classes of people under various forms of federal legislation such as the ADA, Title VII, and the FMLA. While these laws serve an effective purpose of protecting employees, they also prevent an employer from effectively screening out or terminating potentially risky employees.

The role of legal counsel is essential to help minimize the potential liability an employer can face in relation to workplace violence. Legal counsel will be able to aid in the implementation of pre-employment screening procedures that do not violate an individual's privacy rights but also provide sufficient information to the employer regarding the potential hire's threat level. Counsel will also be able to assist during a potential incident through mediation and ensuring the company's policy is effective, and after an incident has occurred, counsel will be able to ensure that a potential lawsuit is avoided or properly handled. Until an actual statutory duty is established, inconsistency will be the norm in countering and responding to workplace violence.

It is often said that the greatest catalyst for change is tragedy. It is by the many tragedies that have occurred in America's workplaces that this statement has been proven true. These tragedies and their subsequent effects show how crucial it is for employers to take action and put into place prevention programs—such as policies, procedures, and threat management resources to identify potential risks—to deal with potential violence in a proactive manner. Judgments are minimized when legal counsel, as part of the multi-disciplinary threat management team, weighs the various legal considerations mentioned, balancing that with specific knowledge of the law and a program for violence prevention.

Notes

1 ASIS International, *Workplace Violence Prevention and Response Guidelines* (2005), at 14.
2 Unless it violates Title VII by discriminating and creates a hostile work environment. U.S. Equal Opportunity Commission, available at: www.eeoc.gov/laws/statutes/titlevii.cfm.
3 *Bauer v. Sampson*, 261 F.3d 775 (9th Cir 2001).
4 29 U.S.C. § 651.
5 29 U.S.C. §654(a)(1).
6 29 U.S.C §654(a)(2).
7 Prevention of Workplace Violence in Healthcare and Social Assistance, Occupational Safety and Health Administration, January 7, 2016, F.R. Doc No. 2016–29197, available at: www.osha.gov/pls/oshaweb/owadisp.show_document?p_table=FEDERAL_REGISTER&p_id=27581.
8 *Nat'l Realty & Constr. Co. v. OSHRC* 489 F.2d 1257 (D.C. 1973).
9 *Franklin v. The Monadnock Co.* 151 Cal. App. 4th 252 (2nd Dist. Ct. App. 2007).
10 United States Department of Labor, State Plan Adoption of OSHA's Revised Reporting Requirements (29 CFR 1904.39), available at: www.osha.gov/recordkeeping2014/state_adoption_table.html
11 *Fla. Retail Fed'n, Inc. v. AG of Fla* 576 F.Supp 2d 1281, 1298 (N.D. Fla 2008).
12 29 U.S.C. §667(a).
13 *Ramsey Winch, Inc v. Henry* 555 F.3d 1199 (10th Cir. 2009).
14 Ibid. at 1202, citing 21 Okla. Stat. §§1289.7(a) & 1290.22.
15 www.parking.org/wp-content/uploads/2016/01/TPP-2014-03-Guns-In-the-Lot.pdf.
16 www.dir.ca.gov/dosh/dosh_publications/IIPP.html#30. The IIPP does not specifically address workplace violence.
17 Cal. Lab. Code §§142, 6307, 6308.
18 1 Littler Mendelson's *The National Employer* § 30.3.
19 Wash. Admin. Code §296-832-100.
20 *Johns v. Unemployment Comp. Bd. of Review*, 87 A.3d 1006 (Comm. Ct. Penn. 2014).
21 Sampson, Richard T., Topazian, Johnathan R., Violence in the workplace, *For the Defense* (December 1996), at 20, 22.
22 *Jacobs v. Experts, Inc.* U.S. Dist. LEXIS 125244§ 2016.

23 Fourth Amendment, Legal Information Institute, Cornell University Law School, (last visited February 22, 2017), available at: www.law.cornell.edu/constitution/fourth_amendment. ("The right of the people to be secure in their persons, houses, papers, and effects, against unreasonable searches and seizures, shall not be violated, and no warrants shall issue, but upon probable cause, supported by oath or affirmation, and particularly describing the place to be searched, and the persons or things to be seized.")

24 *Plante v. Gonzalez*, 575 F.2d 1119, 1132 (5th Cir. 1978).

25 *Nat'l Treasury Employees Union v. U.S. Dept. of Treasury*, 25 F.3d 237, 242 (5th Cir. 1994).

26 *Nat'l Treasury Employees Union*, 25 F.3d at 244 (5th Cir. 1994).

27 Ibid. at 244.

28 Ibid.

29 *O'Connor v. Ortega*, 480 U.S. 709, 725 (1987).

30 Ibid. at 726.

31 Alvarez, Gregory T., Ruff, Jason E., Private-sector employees and workplace privacy in the electronic era, *New Jersey Lawyer*, August, 24 (2007).

32 *K-Mart Corp. Store No. 7441 v. Trotti*, 677 S.W.2d 632 (Tex. App. – Houston [1st Dist.] 1984).

33 *Doe v. Kohn Nast & Graf, P.C.*, 866 F.Supp. 190 (E.D. Pa. 1994).

34 *Acosta v. Scott Labor LLC*, 377 F. Supp. 2d 647, 651 (N.D. Ill. 2005).

35 Alvarez, *supra* note 9, at 24, 26. See 18 U.S.C. § 2510(5)(a); 18 U.S.C. § 2511(2)(a)(i); 18 U.S.C. § 2511(2)(d), and Stored Communications Act 1986.

36 White, Jennifer Heidt, Text message monitoring after Quon v. Arch Wireless: What private employers need to know about the Stored Communications Act and an employee's right to privacy, 5 *Shidler Journal of Law, Commerce & Technology* 19, 12 (2009).

37 § 1:3.Structure of the ADA—Subchapter I [Title I]: Employment, Legal Almanac: The Americans With Disabilities Act § 1:3 (hereinafter ADA § 1:3.)

38 ADA § 1:3.

39 § 1:9.Disabled persons, Legal Almanac: The Americans With Disabilities Act § 1:9. ("Covered physical or mental disabilities may include visual, speech or hearing impairments, orthopedic conditions, epilepsy, cerebral palsy, muscular dystrophy, multiple sclerosis, cancer, heart disease, diabetes, mental retardation, emotional illness, certain learning disabilities, AIDS/HIV disease, tuberculosis, past drug addiction, and alcoholism.") (hereinafter ADA § 1:9.)

40 ADA § 1:9.

41 *McCarthy ex rel. Travis v. Hawkins*, 381 F.3d 407, 431 (5th Cir. 2004).

42 *Bd. of Trustees of Univ. of Alabama v. Garrett*, 531 U.S. 356, 357 (2001).

43 *Hennigh v. City of Shawnee*, 155 F.3d 1249, 1253 (10th Cir. 1998).

44 U.S. Const. amend. XIV, §1. ("All persons born or naturalized in the United States, and subject to the jurisdiction thereof, are citizens of the United States and of the state wherein they reside. No state shall make or enforce any law which shall abridge the privileges or immunities of citizens of the United States; nor shall any state deprive any person of life, liberty, or property, without due process of law; nor deny to any person within its jurisdiction the equal protection of the laws.")

45 Steptoe, Johnson PLLC, 15 No. 9 W. Va. Emp. L. Letter 1 (March 2010).

46 Ibid.

47 29 U.S.C §§151 to 169.

48 3 U.S.C.A. § 411 (West).

49 Ibid.

50 § 8.11.Hostile work environment—Elements, 16A Colo. Prac., Emp. L. & Prac. Handbook § 8.11 (2016–2017 ed.) (hereinafter Hostile Work Environment).

51 Hostile Work Environment.

52 Ibid.

53 Ibid.

54 Beaver, Stephen J., Beyond the exclusivity rule: Employer's liability for workplace violence, 81 *Marquette Law Review*, 103, 104–105 (1997).

55 Ibid. at 105.

56 Ibid. at 106.

57 Beaver, *supra* note 1, at 106.
58 *Faragher v. City of Boca Raton*, 118 S.Ct. 2275, 2286 (1998).
59 Ibid. at 2286.
60 Beaver, *supra* note 1, at 108.
61 Ibid. at 108.
62 Ibid. at 110.
63 Beaver, *supra* note 1, at 110.
64 Ibid. at 117.
65 *Faragher*, 118 S.Ct. at 2286.
66 Ibid. at 2290.
67 Ibid. at 2293.
68 *Doe v. XYC*, 887 A.2d. 1156, 1158 (App. Div. 2005)
69 Ibid. at 1158.
70 United States Department of Labor, *DOL Workplace Violence Program – Appendices* (last visited February 22, 2017), available at: www.dol.gov/oasam/hrc/policies/dol-workplace-violence-program-appendices.htm.
71 Beaver, *supra* note 1, at 115.
72 Ibid. at 116.
73 Ibid. at 114.
74 Ibid. at 126.
75 Riley, Kyle, Employer TROS are all the rage: A new approach to workplace violence, 4 *Nevada Law Journal* 1, 4 (2003).
76 Ibid. at 8.

6 The Employee Assistance Program (EAP) and Its Role in the Management of Workplace Threats

Whether in-house, external, or some combination of both, employee assistance programs (EAPs) play an important role in the threat management process. In organizations that have such programs, EAP professionals are integral members of the threat management team (TMT). In this chapter we will discuss EAP programs and how they assist in mitigating threatening behavior and threats.

The development of EAP programs can trace their origin to the alcohol abuse prevention programs from many years ago. Today, while alcohol abuse prevention is still an important issue, these programs have evolved and have added other programs that fall under the category of employee "health and wellness." It is not unusual for EAP professionals to counsel on drug abuse, financial and legal problems, mental health, and personal problems, which impact employees not only personally but professionally. Invariably, these "personal" problems if not addressed have a "ripple effect" on the workplace, potentially impacting other co-workers and ultimately affecting productivity and causing discord in the workplace.

EAPs, as part of their ever-expanding role, have since gotten involved in the prevention of workplace violence. EAP professionals many times are the "go to" folks for managers who are looking for help in dealing with a difficult employee. They will counsel managers as to how to mediate issues between employees who cannot get along, and/or have engaged with employees who have displayed behaviors which are concerning and have the potential for violence. They also have intervened and counseled on issues of domestic violence that may have come to light from an employee who has confided in management that they are dealing with violence at home and are looking for help. They play an important role in assessing an individual for the potential for violence: whether he or she is a potential threat to commit violence in the workplace. Similarly to the TMT concept, they work with individuals and management to mitigate behavior which is concerning to co-workers and others in the workplace. As TMT members, they provide counsel and expertise to the TMT from a mental health perspective, depending on the facts and circumstances in a given situation.

EAP professionals can be from a number of different backgrounds. They can be licensed clinical social workers and/or trained psychologists or psychiatrists; in some cases they might be peer counselors who have undergone specialized training and who refer clients to clinical professionals. They can also be individuals who possess advanced degrees in behavioral health.

In most instances, referral to an EAP professional is done on a voluntary basis; however, in some cases employees might be encouraged to seek EAP counsel by a co-worker, a manager, human resources (HR), or a union representative. Depending on the situation, treatment by an EAP professional may be made mandatory and a condition of employment if the employee does not avail himself or herself of the services that they provide. Generally, this mandatory EAP occurs when there has been a threat of violence, an individual's work fitness is in question, and/or there is a question of alcohol or drug abuse.

Confidentiality

EAP professionals are bound by strict confidentiality laws, and no one in an organization will know that an individual is being seen by them unless permission is granted by the patient. Confidentiality, however, can be denied in specific circumstances, for example, if an individual poses a threat to himself or others, or if there is a duty to warn based upon knowledge the EAP professional has obtained while treating the client that he/she is mandated to report, for example, to the person threatened or to law enforcement. EAP professionals can be mandatory reporters in certain instances, if it is disclosed that there has been sexual abuse of a child, for example (Newman, 2003).

A person's employer will receive no information from the EAP professional except that to which the patient agrees in writing. Usually, EAP providers will give employers statistical information regarding usage and demographics, but never specifics about names or what issues were discussed. If an employee is under special circumstances, such as rehabilitation for substance abuse, domestic violence, or any other program mandated by the company, state, or regulatory agency, the employee may have to sign a specific release of information document before the employer receives information other than that stated earlier (Newman, 2003).

For example, workplace violence incidents, including threatening behavior and/or threats, may lead to employer-mandated fitness for duty evaluations or other assessments, to include a formal threat assessment by a qualified forensic professional, which generally include provisions for direct reports to the employer about whether the subject employee can safely return to work.

While we often think of EAP professionals as dealing with employee problems which may prevent a violent incident from occurring, they also provide valuable services, should the unthinkable happen, after a violent event occurs. They can provide critical incident stress debriefing services to management and employees and counsel employees in both the short and the long term on the nature of trauma and how to mitigate its effects, which ultimately can improve their work and home life.

EAP Programs and Threat Management

EAP professionals play an important role in the mitigation and management of threatening behavior and threats by being an integral part of the threat management process. In organizations that have some type of TMT, their role is to assist the team in assessing threatening behaviors and threats. As stated in the ASIS/Society for Human Resource Management (SHRM) *Workplace Violence Prevention and Intervention* (2011), the role of EAP professionals in threat management may include the following:

1. As part of efforts to resolve an incident, an employee who has been found to have engaged in concerning behavior may be referred to EAP for counseling, as part of a remedial or corrective plan.
2. EAP may be engaged to provide psychological counseling to employees or workgroups affected by a threat or violent incident.
3. While normally bound by obligations of confidentially, EAP personnel involved in counseling an employee may receive information that triggers an obligation to warn the employer of a threat posed by the employee.

In some organizations, EAP may be asked to conduct an initial threat assessment on an individual who may pose a risk. EAP professionals may be called upon to assist in the following situations.

The Employee Who Is Troubled by Personal Issues

A manager and/or HR personnel would contact the EAP professional for assistance in handling the troubled employee. Many times, someone dealing with personal issues could neglect their professional responsibilities, which would lead to job performance issues and could lead to some form of discipline by management. EAP would deal with the employee's emotional state, while management would deal with any disciplinary issues that might arise. By working as a team and coordinating efforts, they could decide on an appropriate course of action which would benefit not only the worker but also the organization, with the goal of helping the employee and making him productive on the job again. Management, working with the EAP professional, would discuss the best way to proceed, and get the employee to seek treatment, which can be done in a number of ways:

- Advise the employee that help is available and get him or her to seek counseling voluntarily
- Emphasize that there will be no repercussions if he or she chooses not to see the counselor
- Formally refer the employee to EAP based upon already established policy if the organization has such a policy

As part of a larger job performance improvement process, the employee can be asked to agree to EAP counseling as part of a job performance review-and-improvement process. If this is agreed to by the employee, as a manager you may do the following:

- Have the employee sign a limited release of information (ROI) to allow the employer to track attendance at counseling sessions
- Refer the employee to an EAP counselor, per company procedure
- Document whether the employee attends counseling sessions or not

If allegations of threatening behavior or threats are involved and EAP is contacted by management, the EAP professional might recommend that as a manager you contact your TMT to bring multi-disciplinary input and recommendations to bear early in the process. It is possible that your company's security personnel, or others on the TMT, have had some dealings with the same employee on this or other related issues, and knowing all facts and circumstances in totality might dictate a way forward.

When threatening behavior or some type of threat is reported

EAP Consultation

Depending on the situation and the nature of the threat, an employee who has been threatened verbally or who has been exposed to threatening behavior may approach a manager with information related to what has occurred. Take immediate action to protect the victim(s) from further harm or retaliation. It may be necessary to convene the TMT (which would include EAP) to discuss the situation and determine appropriate action to take regarding the perpetrator. This could include a formal referral for EAP counseling (see earlier), referral to community resources for "anger management" treatment, taking certain security precautions, and a variety of HR options such as putting the perpetrator on administrative leave, limiting access to the job site, and so on. Discussion with the TMT can help you sort out the appropriate response.

Depending on the seriousness of the issue, EAP can arrange for a threat assessment to be done on the perpetrator by a qualified forensic clinician. Not all clinicians are qualified to do this kind of assessment, so be sure to screen your clinician. A threat assessment by a clinician will likely outline and test for certain risk factors for violence. The more risk factors a person exhibits, the higher the potential for violence from that person. While no assessment is foolproof, it is an opinion based upon the best available facts and circumstances found through investigation; the results must be correlated with other experiences with the person in question to determine the veracity of the threat.

Conflict Resolution

Another role that EAP professionals play is in the mediation of conflicts within work groups, between employees, and between managers and employees. These situations typically do not reach the level of threat management, but they can, and are often initiated by a manager or HR to deal with a particular issue or conflict. This mediation can often bring the underlying issues to light and can foster a less toxic work environment. Conflicts frequently result from misunderstandings, misperceptions, and prejudices. Once these issues are brought into the open in a safe environment, with a qualified professional, the parties can gain a deeper understanding of one another.

Training (Newman, 2003)

EAP professionals can provide training workshops on workplace cooperation and conflict resolution as well as workplace violence prevention. This type of training would underscore the organization's expectations regarding employee conduct and professionalism. Some areas that EAP might be able to discuss include:

- Overcoming conflict with better communication
- Gender communication (especially if conflict involved both men and women)
- Creating a positive workplace environment (or other attitude-related topic)
- Harassment awareness (including other forms of harassment beyond sexual harassment)
- Cultural awareness, commonly referred to as diversity training
- Customer service (if the incident or threat involved a customer, including an internal customer)
- Workplace violence prevention, awareness, and procedures (especially if it has been a long time since the last such workshop)

After a Critical Incident (Death or Perceived Threat to Life) (Newman, 2003)

EAP Consultation

Call your EAP professional (or alternative provider) for counselors trained in critical incident stress management (CISM) procedures. They can help ensure the emotional health of your employees through all the phases of response.

Organizational Development Consulting

For an objective post-incident assessment of how your company responded and what parts of the threat management program proved effective, contact your EAP and ask for a consultant to review the incident. After any incident, it is very important to review what worked and what did not, and to make appropriate adjustments to policies and procedures.

Threat Management: Threat Assessment versus Fitness for Duty

What is a threat assessment, and what role does EAP have in determining level of risk? Threat assessment refers to the determination of whether an individual poses a risk to himself and others in the workplace. It is a part of the threat management process. When a threat has been made, or if threatening behavior is observed and reported, depending on the specific facts and circumstances, the following may occur:

- TMT determines that employee may represent a threat of harm to others in the workplace, and refers to the EAP
- HR secures employee signature on ROI between EAP and Company Medical and notifies employee of EAP evaluation requirement. HR provides EAP with the signed ROI
- Security provides EAP with a copy of the security investigation with other employee names redacted so they have as much background as possible to determine the nature and context of the threatening behavior or threat

When the employee is seen by the EAP professional, in some cases, it is clear after initial evaluation that the employee does not represent an imminent threat of harm, and the employee is cleared for return to work.

However, in other situations, the EAP professional will require additional medical evaluation from either:

- Another type of medical professional
- A former treating provider for the employee (such as when a patient has stopped taking their medication of record)
- A chemical dependency professional
- A forensic specialist

If additional treatment is indicated, EAP will "case-manage" the employee treatment until such time as the professionals involved agree that the employee does not represent a threat of harm in the workplace. It is important to realize that a formal threat assessment is not the same as a fitness for duty assessment.

Fitness for Duty

Fitness for duty refers to behavior in the workplace that prevents an employee from performing essential requirements of their job.

- HR, management, and legal concur that employee appears to be medically unfit for duty.
- Management would contact EAP, who would refer the employee to health services or outside provider. Information should be provided to the examining physician indicating the specific behaviors which give rise to medical concern
- If the case is strictly psychiatric, HR may secure an employee release of information between the EAP vendor and the organization's health services or physician
- Company health services and the EAP mental health professional coordinate, and the initial evaluation is conducted

In some cases, it is clear after initial evaluation that the behavior cited is not the result of a medical condition, and the employee is cleared for return to work.

In some cases, medical or the EAP professional will require additional medical evaluation from:

- a specialized medical professional in the community, or
- a former treating provider for the employee (such as when a patient has stopped taking their medication of record), or
- a chemical dependency professional

It is important to know that in both a formal threat assessment and fitness for duty, actions facilitated and coordinated by EAP are an adjunct to, not in lieu of, any corrective action that may result from an individual's behavior in the workplace.

Drug-Free Workplace

Another way that EAP can assist is in the area of drug-free workplace referrals. This can also be considered when unusual behavior is observed, and/or behavior which may suggest some type of impairment. EAP, in consultation with outside specialists, test the employee for any chemical dependency, and depending on the situation, a treatment plan is developed and the employee may be monitored for a period of time.

Working as Part of the TMT

It is important that TMT members develop a close relationship with your EAP partners when discussing cases that may be referred to the team. Confidentiality may prevent them from discussing case specifics, but their insight and experience will be invaluable to the overall assessment by the team. Many times, as we have seen, there is some confusion between threat assessments, which are conducted by an EAP professional in conjunction with a forensic doctor, someone who is experienced in issues of dangerousness relating to violence in the workplace, and fitness for duty, which often manifests itself in unusual or bizarre behavior that frightens co-workers and may be a sign of some type of mental health issue which may limit job performance as opposed to a risk to the workplace. Education on this issue is key so that the right examination is requested by managers and HR in dealing with this type of behavior.

An important aspect of these examinations is that the mental health professional who performs the examination has the most complete information possible, which will aid him or her in asking the right questions to determine either issue. Many times these mental health professionals, lacking information from the company about the facts and circumstances surrounding the referral, cannot formulate pertinent questions which would allow them to get to the heart of the matter. As a result, a less than complete examination could occur.

EAP professionals play a multi-faceted role in the prevention of workplace violence, from dealing with employee concerns, to management referrals due to employee behavior, and ultimately as an active participant in the organization's TMTs—all under the umbrella of providing a safe working environment for all employees.

References

Newman, Paul (2003) Employee assistance programs, in Elliott, J.F. (ed.), *Workplace Violence Prevention: A Practical Guide* (2 vols), Vancouver, BC: Specialty Technical Publishers.

7 Risk Assessment in Domestic Violence and Stalking Cases

Pamela A. Paziotopoulos

Domestic Violence Statistics

Domestic violence has become an epidemic in our society. The overwhelming majority of adult domestic violence victims are women, and the perpetrators are men. One in four women will report domestic abuse in their lifetime. For each minute that passes, 24 people are victims of intimate partner violence. Three or more women are murdered by their boyfriends or husbands every day. In fact, domestic violence homicides account for about one-third of all female homicides. Although anyone can experience intimate partner violence, women aged 18 to 34 are at the greatest risk of becoming victims of domestic violence.[1] Unfortunately, most domestic violence incidents are left unreported, or they are not given the serious attention they deserve. In certain cases, these situations can turn fatal … fast. In this chapter, we will discuss how to identify the risk factors present in these cases before they escalate. Lethality or threat assessments in these types of cases can be an essential and critical tool in preventing future violence. These instruments are akin to taking a snapshot of the situation that would enable one to predict how much time is pending before an offender commits an act of violence.

Defining Domestic Violence

Domestic violence is defined as *the deliberate use of emotional, psychological, physical, financial, and sexual abuse in intimate adult or teen relationships in order to control the partner.*[2] Domestic violence is used by the perpetrator to control the victim. This is accomplished by using tactics such as fear, guilt, shame, and intimidation. When the victim terminates the relationship and thus breaks the cycle of violence, the relationship has the potential to be fatal. It is well known that in most domestic violence homicides, the victims have communicated recently to the perpetrator that their relationship has terminated, or they have already exited the relationship. Much of domestic violence is a form of "separation assault." They are deliberate acts, conducted when the woman leaves or says she is going to leave. The perpetrator responds by terrorizing her into remaining in the relationship.[3] According to Martha Mahoney's article in the *Michigan Law Review*, at least half of women who leave their abusers are followed, harassed, or attacked by them.[4] Violence quickly escalates after the separation. Many women who are killed by their husbands are killed soon after they separate. According to an article by Susan J. Dansie, the risk of death for a victim once separated increases fivefold.[5]

Domestic Violence and the Workplace

During this time of separation, domestic violence often infiltrates the workplace. The offender might not know where the victim resides after the separation, but he knows where she works. Thus, employers become critical players in preventing harm to victims and to their other employees. Note: abusers regularly stalk, threaten, harass, and/or physically harm their victims in the workplace. The National Institute for Occupational Safety and Health defines workplace violence as violent acts, including physical assaults and threats of assaults, directed toward persons at work or on duty. Workplace violence ranges from offensive or threatening language to homicide, and it may include domestic violence, sexual violence, sexual harassment or sexual assault, dating violence, and stalking.[6] According to ASIS/ Society for Human Resource Management (SHRM), workplace violence is a "spectrum of behaviors—including overt acts of violence, threats, and other conduct—that generates a reasonable concern for safety from violence, where a nexus exists between the behavior and the physical safety of employees and others on-site, or off-site when related to the organization."[7]

Integrating sound workplace policies and procedures can have a very positive influence on the victim's life, on the lives of employees, on the community, and on the workplace's bottom line.

Examples of Domestic Violence Infiltrating the Workplace

Domestic violence victims can change their residence, but they cannot change the location of their workplace. This fact makes their workplace a target for the abuser. The power and control tactics that were used in the shared residence are now taken to the workplace. The abuser is well aware of the victim's travel patterns and work hours. This makes it very easy for the abuser to target the victim while at work. Can we predict whether an abuser will act out violently or not? There are several red flags or lethality indicators often present in these types of cases. The following cases are examples of how lethal abuse can infiltrate the workplace.

Cynthia Bischof

Cynthia Bischof was a very successful commercial real estate broker. After she terminated her relationship of many years with her boyfriend, he began stalking her—ultimately taking her life in the parking lot of her employer after she left her workplace in Elmhurst, Illinois on March 7, 2008. She tried on numerous occasions to bring charges against her abuser, but despite the protective orders and his violations, he was allowed out on bond. She asked the judge to require the offender to wear a global positioning system (GPS) monitoring bracelet, but the judge stated it was not within his capability. Cynthia took all the necessary legal steps. She reported violations to the police, appeared in court, and cooperated with law enforcement and the prosecution. However, it was not enough to save her life. On August 4, 2008, Governor Rod Blagojevich signed legislation that allows courts to order an abuser to wear a GPS tracking device as a condition of bail in instances when a restraining order has been violated.[8]

In a domestic violence case, if a domestic abuser is arrested for violating a restraining order and appeals for bail, the Cindy Bischof Law requires that the abuser must undergo a risk assessment evaluation that gives the court authority to require a GPS device be worn if bail is granted. In addition, the court must order the abuser to be evaluated by a partner abuse intervention program while ordering the respondent to follow all recommendations. The law further establishes it as a new offense when the restraining order is violated by the abuser's failure to attend and complete a partner abuse intervention program.

The new law adds at least a $200 additional fine to every penalty regarding a violation of a restraining order conviction. The fines are deposited into the newly established Domestic Violence Surveillance Fund. Detailed information about the Cindy Bischof Law, as well as whether or not this effective prevention tool is available in your state, can be found at www. cindysmemorial.org.

Nordstrom Shooting

On November 28, 2014, 22-year-old Nadia Ezaldein was working her seasonal job in the accessories department of the North Michigan Avenue Nordstrom in downtown Chicago, on the eve of Black Friday, one of the busiest shopping nights of the year. At about 8:30 p.m., a man by the name of Marcus Dee walked up to the counter, exchanged a few words with Nadia, and then shot her in the head before turning the gun on himself.[9] Fear and chaos ensued. After hearing those two gunshots, Nordstrom shoppers frantically ran around the mall trying to find exits, tripping and knocking over one another. They feared for their safety. People had no idea what had happened or why. Was anybody injured? Killed? Was this an act of terror? Was it random, or was this a decisive attack?

As the police responded to the situation and more information trickled in, it became clear that it was in fact a decisive attack. Marcus Dee had a purpose in entering Nordstrom that night. He knew he would find Nadia, his ex-girlfriend, working, and he brought a .45-caliber semi-automatic with him. He murdered an innocent woman, someone with whom he had been intimate, before killing himself. What Marcus Dee did that night was bring domestic violence—homicide—to the workplace. This is a tragedy that happens more often than one might think, and a crucial question to ask is: Can something like this be prevented?

Prevention is a key factor to address in domestic violence cases. Often times it can be hard getting to the bottom of these cases, because there is no physical evidence, nor are there any witnesses to the abuse. Initially, the extent of the danger and the risk of an escalation of violence may not be apparent. These factors make it critical that professionals in the field identify the threat as soon as it appears and assess the likelihood of future violence before it reaches a more serious stage. If it is apparent that violence is escalating, the victim could be at risk for serious injury or death.

According to the 2000 Supplemental Homicide Records, women in the United States are murdered by an intimate partner or former partner more often than by an acquaintance or stranger. In fact, 30% of American women who are killed are murdered by an intimate or ex-partner.[10] How does this happen? Do these partners just snap, or are there pre-incident indicators?

Lethality Indicators

Professionals in the threat assessment field recognize that in these situations people do not "snap." Rather, there are warning signs and pre-incident indicators that point to the possibility of or the degree of violence. For example, in the Nordstrom shooting case, there were many indicators revealing that serious harm could be inflicted upon the victim, Nadia Ezaldein. An analysis of the history of their relationship disclosed the high level of risk that the violence and threats had reached. Unfortunately, the numerous "lethality indicators" in this case were not identified, and thus no plan was created for preventing this tragedy.

Many of the pre-incident indicators seen in the Nordstrom shooting case parallel those seen in other domestic violence cases. Throughout the relationship, Marcus Dee physically abused Nadia. In December 2013, he threatened her by inserting a handgun into her mouth. That incident led to a hospital visit for Nadia, after which she terminated the relationship. Marcus continued to harass Nadia and her family after the relationship ended, often calling and threatening to hurt or kill himself. Nadia changed her number at least three times to try to shake his persistence and harassment, but to no avail. She was going to request an order of protection but was threatened by Marcus on numerous occasions and "warned" not to pursue any court remedies.[11]

Situations like this happen frequently in intimate partner violence cases, where the victim feels she has no other options. As for the abuser, often he will take the harassment and violence one step further by bringing it to the workplace. In this manner, the abuser is able to exercise even more power and control. He knows when and where the victim will be working, where she parks her car, and often can enter the workplace with minimal restrictions. When violence is brought to the workplace, the potential for harm to other employees increases. This is where threat assessment becomes an instrumental tool in preventing and minimizing workplace violence. Threat assessment, or threat management teams within the organization, should conduct risk assessments in cases where employees are involved in domestic violence or have become victims of stalking.

Threat Assessments

In situations of intimate partner violence, the first priority is to identify the threat, assess the possibility of subsequent violence, and determine the best way to intervene. The goal for security personnel or anyone conducting a threat assessment is to determine the potential danger early enough to enable them to be in a position to prevent or defuse the situation.

Assessments can take a number of forms—including the detailed and psychologically sophisticated assessments known as "threat assessments," "fitness for duty evaluations," and/ or "lethality assessments." These assessments should be performed by trained professionals. However, others such as non-expert managers and co-workers can and should be willing to start the assessment process if necessary and consult experts when deemed appropriate.

Threat assessments can discern (1) the exact nature and context of a threat and/or threatening behavior; (2) the identified target; (3) the apparent motivation behind the threat; and (4) a perpetrator's background, including work history, criminal record, mental health history, and past behavior on the job.[12] Threat assessments can make the difference between life and death in domestic violence situations and are crucial for maintaining the welfare of everyone within the workplace setting. They are used "to assist those in law enforcement in determining how to evaluate a victim's case in light of known past events, rather than to help the trier of fact determine whether a particular defendant is guilty of a domestic violence-related homicide."

Lethality assessments help the abused women themselves—they want to know how much risk their situation presents in order to act accordingly; provide evidence of dangerousness for civil and criminal justice proceedings and give advocates and first responders the ability to assess risk with abused women; provide for the need for judges, probation officers, and other criminal justice practitioners to have an accurate system to determine potential danger; and cite factors that have been researched and formed to distinguish cases of intimate partner violence from cases of intimate partner homicide of women.

It has been researched and concluded that there are indeed factors that can distinguish cases of intimate partner violence from cases of intimate partner homicide for women.[13] The greater the number of predictors, the greater the potential for the batterer to commit a homicide or engage in potentially lethal behaviors.[14]

Jacquelyn Campbell and the Danger Assessment

Jacquelyn Campbell is one of the foremost leaders in research into domestic violence and violence against women, designed the Danger Assessment in 1986. The purpose of this assessment is to determine the "likelihood of lethality or near lethality occurring in a case of intimate partner violence." The Danger Assessment consists of two parts: a calendar and a 20-item scoring instrument.

The calendar is used to determine the severity and frequency of abuse within the past year. The victim marks approximate dates of abuse and ranks the severity of abuse from one to five (one=slap, pushing, no injuries and/or lasting pain through five=use of weapon, wounds from weapon).

The first part of the Danger Assessment is less focused on the accuracy of the dates of phys-ical abuse and more about raising awareness of the violent situations taking place. It is a way for the victim to start realizing the extent of the danger and reduce denial.

Next is the 20-item instrument, which is a series of yes/no questions about risk factors associated with intimate partner homicide. The instrument systematically weighs the responses to determine the level of danger the victim may have reached regarding intimate partner homicide.[15]

This assessment, along with others that will be discussed later in this chapter, takes into account as much information as possible about the intimate partner violence occurring, assesses potential risk factors, and determines to what extent the victim is in danger.

Assessing and Understanding the Situation

When assessing intimate partner abuse cases, the goal is to recognize this kind of behavior, document it, and then take a proactive approach to identify the potential problem early enough to prevent or defuse the situation.

If the victim is ready to discuss the abusive relationship, it is highly recommended that someone helping to assess the situation documents in writing what is discussed. In this way, he or she can determine whether certain pre-incident indicators are present and to what extent they pose a serious risk. In assessing threat, when the right questions are asked early enough, steps can be taken to alleviate the potential threat of severe and/or lethal violence.

Although it is important to assess any harassment or violence that occurs in the workplace, those involved in the situation should not limit questions to only work-related incidents. Too often, interviewers limit their questions to the particular incident that occurred at the work-place. For instance, if the abuser has called the victim, the interviewer may simply ask about the call. "When did it occur? What was said?". Asking the who, what, when, where, how, and why questions gets quick results for purposes of documenting the incident, but it does not touch the underlying issues. Workplace violence is often an extension of abuse already occurring in the home. Employers need to meet the victim's situation with prompt and supportive attention. This reaction will validate the victim's concerns about safety as well as showing the employer's involvement and concern with the matter.

Pre-Incident Indicators

The following is a list of pre-incident indicators that should be incorporated into a risk assessment in an intimate partner violence case.[16]

Status of the Relationship

"Have you told the abuser that you intend to leave this relationship, or have you already terminated it?" This question is a key indicator of increased risk of threat, and it is one that should be asked right away. As shown in the Nordstrom shooting, severe threats and har-assment continued after Nadia Ezaldein ended the relationship. The perpetrator persistently harassed not only Nadia but also her family members. He threatened to kill himself if she went to the authorities. Termination or intended termination of the relationship is a precursor to most domestic violence homicides and a clear indication that escalation of violence is a real possibility.

In Campbell's risk assessment validation study released in 2005, she notes the association found between intimate partner homicide and estrangement. Referring to research conducted in 1995, she explains that the combination of physical and legal separation poses the most risk.

This research theorizes that "male partners are threatened by loss of control over the relationship when women announce their decision to separate, and some men will stop at nothing to regain control, including femicide (the murder of women)."[17]

If the victim answers "yes" to this first question, it is imperative that the employer helps the victim establish a safety plan for home and work and begins adjusting the victim's work schedule and routine to ensure protection when arriving, while at work, and when leaving. When the abuser loses immediate access to the victim after termination of the relationship, the controlling behavior of the abuser reveals itself in public rather than in private. This behavior can include phone harassment, violating an order of protection, and showing up at a victim's workplace.

Reaction to Breakup

Along the same lines as asking about the status of the relationship, if the victim ended the relationship, it is important to assess the abuser's reaction. Did the abuser try to force the victim to remain in the relationship? Was there a physical struggle when trying to leave? Did the abuser become obsessed with finding the victim? These types of reactions are a way for the abuser to impede the victim from getting help. Experts characterize this as "interfering with the victim's help-seeking behavior." At this time, as the abuser fears losing control, violence will generally escalate in order to increase the victim's fear.

Stalking

The next key step in threat assessment is to examine the kind of behaviors the abuser exhibits once the relationship has ended. Stalking is a behavior often seen after the abuser feels he has lost control and access to the victim. It is defined as

> harassing, unwanted, and/or threatening behavior that causes the victim to fear for his or her safety or the safety of a family member, or would cause a reasonable person in a similar situation to fear for his or her safety. It can include, but is not limited to: following or spying on a person, appearing at a person's home or work, showing up at a place where the perpetrator has no reason to be, waiting at places in order to make unwanted contact with the victim or to monitor the victim, leaving unwanted items and gifts for the victim, and posting information or spreading rumors about the victim on the internet, in a public place, or by word of mouth.[18]

Stalking is a pattern of behavior that makes you feel afraid, nervous, harassed, or in danger. It is when someone repeatedly contacts you, follows you, sends you things, talks to you when you don't want them to, or threatens you. Stalking behaviors can include:

- Knowing your schedule
- Showing up at places you go
- Sending mail, email, and pictures
- Calling or texting repeatedly
- Contacting you or posting about you on social networking sites (Facebook, Twitter, etc.)
- Writing letters
- Damaging your property
- Creating a website about you
- Sending gifts
- Stealing things that belong to you
- Any other actions to contact, harass, track, or frighten you[19]

Stalking Statistics

- The majority of stalking victims are stalked by someone they know: 61% of female victims and 44% of male victims of stalking are stalked by a current or former intimate partner; 25% of female victims and 32% of male victims are stalked by an acquaintance
- About half of all victims of stalking indicated that they were stalked before the age of 25. About 14% of female victims and 16% of male victims experienced stalking between the ages of 11 and 17

Approaching the victim or showing up in places where the victim did not want them to visit; making unwanted telephone calls; leaving the victim unwanted messages (text or voice); watching or following the victim from a distance; or spying on the victim with a listening device, camera, or GPS were the most commonly reported stalker tactics by both female and male victims of stalking.[20]

According to Campbell, stalking may be an even more common precursor of intimate partner homicide than abuse. A 1999 report by McFarlane, Campbell, and associates found that "stalking and harassment occurred in 70 to 90 percent of 200 actual and attempted femicides in 11 U.S. cities."[21] Clearly, stalking is a red flag for predicting future violence. If the abuser physically assaults, stalks, or displays threatening behavior toward the victim in public places, violence may be escalating. If stalking is happening at the workplace, there are steps employers can take to minimize the risk to their employees. These steps include reviewing existing violence in the workplace policies and procedures, ensuring staff are appropriately screening calls and people entering and leaving the building, passing out a photograph of the stalker to security personnel, and making sure the victim has a safe way of getting to and from work. Safeguards particular to the workplace should be discussed and communicated to the appropriate staff.

Orders of Protection

Often times, if the victim has requested an order of protection against the abuser, the situation has probably elevated to a more serious stage. Knowing how the abuser reacted to the order also reveals the severity of the situation. If he violated the order, the criminal justice system is probably not seen by the abuser as an obstacle. The same goes for resisting arrest. If the abuser has ever been arrested for a crime involving domestic violence or for any other crime, he may have resisted arrest. Again, this shows that the abuser probably does not see the system as a deterrent.

It is important to note an order of protection when assessing the level of threat. However, in cases where the victim has not sought an order of protection, this does not necessarily indicate that the risk of severe and/or lethal violence is not high. It is vital to ask the victim whether she has contemplated seeking an order of protection. Perhaps she wanted to but was too afraid of retaliation and violence by the abuser. In the case of Nadia Ezaldein, she attempted to get an order of protection but then backed out of it due to harassment and threats of suicide by her abuser. Her fear of the abuser's response is an important indicator that there may be an increased likelihood of violence.

Drugs and Alcohol

The notion that abusers physically and mentally abuse because they are under the influence of drugs and alcohol is a greatly mistaken belief. Substance abuse is not a clear indicator of domestic violence or homicide. Some abusers have never used drugs, while some drug addicts have never abused their spouses or partners. If drugs and alcohol are a part of the situation, it may mean that the violence could intensify if the abuser has recently used drugs or alcohol. It is imperative to inquire in these situations whether the abuser has "upped" or increased their usage. In other words, ascertain whether they used to drink one beer daily after work, whereas now they are getting completely intoxicated every night. Asking questions about the abuser's drug use and determining whether the abuse gets more severe when he is under the influence can be vital information in a threat assessment.

Guns

Having access to guns is an important factor to know when engaging in threat assessment. In a domestic violence study conducted in 1996, the research shows that "firearms were nearly two times more likely to be used in intimate partner femicides than other femicides."[22] If the abuser has a gun, the threat assessment professional should ask whether or not the weapon was recently acquired. If it was, it could mean that the abuser has the intention of using it in the near future, increasing the risk of lethality or near-lethality. Recent acquisition of a firearm increases the likelihood of future violence. This is often the case when examining active shooter situations.

Irrespective of Audience

Bringing domestic violence out into the public—such as to the workplace—or doing so in front of children often signifies violence that is spiraling out of control. Be sure to ask the victim if violence is occurring in front of the children. Also, take note of how often the abuser threatens the victim while at work. If the abuser starts appearing at the workplace without regard for what other employees think, this behavior could be a sign that a violent attack—and possibly a fatal one—might be imminent.

Symbolic Violence

To increase fear in the victim, the abuser may destroy something of significance, such as an important award from work, a photograph, or some other memento special to the victim. The abuser may also communicate a threat by sending flowers, a gift, or a hallmark card. These types of gestures to continue the contact when they have been expressly told to "stay away" may be a sign of a serious threat and a heightened risk of violence. If these behaviors are present, there may be an escalation of violence or a near-future threat.

Strangulation

Strangulation is defined as the obstruction of blood vessels and/or airflow in the neck leading to asphyxia. Putting hands around the victim's neck and attempting strangulation is considered a very high indicator of future violence. Also, it is often the reason for a domestic violence-related homicide (http://classic.austlii.edu.au/au/journals/SydLawRw/2014/11.pdf).

Assessment of the Abuser

It is imperative for an individual who is assessing threat to understand that the relationship between the victim and the abuser is a key component to uncovering the likelihood of serious violence. Moreover, it is crucial to address the events surrounding the life of the abuser in order to gain insight into his thought processes, future intentions, and psyche. What is occurring in the abuser's personal and professional life? Is the abuser employed? If so, was he recently demoted or fired? Has he experienced any personal losses or possibly experienced a recent separation or divorce? Inquiries such as these will determine whether or not the abuser's life is on a downward spiral. When the abuser feels "hopeless" or is out of options, then the possibility of a murder/suicide is substantially heightened. If so, the domestic situation may get worse and reach a point of severe violence and/or homicide.

Research reviewed by Campbell in her risk assessment validation study lists characteristics consistently found to be associated with intimate partner violence. These are important to discuss in a threat assessment to evaluate whether they might be a factor in the situation. The research conducted reveals that these characteristics include experiencing violence in the family of origin (either as a child victim of abuse or as a witness to abuse of the mother by a partner), substance abuse, and unemployment.[23]

To understand the current situation between the victim and the abuser, it is also critical to inquire about any past violence and relationships of the abuser. Knowing what kind of abuse and to what degree the abuser has inflicted pain on former victims can indicate whether the risk for severe violence and/or homicide for the current victim is high. Be sure to document every violent act by the abuser, even if the victim claims it was only a small push or shove. Women will sometimes underestimate the act or not see a "push" as a serious threat. Campbell, however, has found in her research that a woman's perception of risk is one of the most important ways to determine risk of assault and re-assault by an intimate partner. Thus, in a threat assessment, it is critical to document all acts of violence. The extreme act of this kind is strangulation, and if the abuser has ever attempted to do this to the victim, the likelihood of future violence is greatly increased.

Suicide

Lastly, assessment of the abuser's state of mind may give clues to escalation of violence. If the abuser is experiencing severe depression or thoughts of suicide, he may act out violently without care for the consequences. The abuser may go so far as to commit a homicide-suicide, in which the abuser kills the victim and then takes his own life. This scenario is what occurred between Nadia Ezaldein and Marcus Dee on that tragic night at Nordstrom in downtown Chicago. Countless threats of suicide occurred before the incident. Marcus decided to bring a gun to Nadia's place of employment and took both their lives. Threat of suicide is a clear pre-incident indicator of future violence and should be taken very seriously. Campbell's research reveals that homicide-suicide represents a significant proportion—27% to 32%—of intimate partner femicides.[24] Thus, evaluating the abuser's state of mind can determine the likelihood that he will end the life of the victim as well as his own. If statements regarding suicide have been made, inquire how specific the abuser was in articulating a suicide plan. Did the plan include murdering the victim too? Did the plan include harming the children? The more specific the plan, the more likely a tragic event may ensue.

Fear

The bottom line in threat assessment is whether the victim fears for her life. If so, it is important to respond to this fear while assuming that there is a chance that violent and/or fatal consequences could occur in the future. Often during threat assessment, the simple questions are overlooked. As discussed earlier, a woman's perception of risk is a critical factor in assessing threat. Thus, questions about how the victim is feeling in these situations can yield important results. Consider questions such as:

- "Are you afraid of the abuser?"
- "Have you ever gone to a domestic violence shelter?"
- "Has the abuser ever physically abused you to the point that you had to seek medical attention?"
- "Do you feel that you are always walking on eggshells?"

Though these are seemingly simple questions, the answers must be incorporated into a thorough threat assessment analysis.

Conclusion

Although every domestic violence situation is unique and should be handled with the utmost respect and privacy for the victim, there are common risk factors that clearly point to the likelihood of extreme violence and/or intimate partner homicide. For a threat assessment professional or someone involved in this kind of situation, determining whether these risk factors pertain to this particular situation can minimize the chance of any harm targeting the victim as well as other individuals (i.e. co-workers) indirectly involved in this situation.

It is important to keep in mind that the initial by-products of domestic violence seeping into the workplace are usually smaller segments of larger, more complicated problems. Those unpleasant or threatening phone calls at work provide little insight into the severity of the situation the abused employee faces. It is important, therefore, to keep in mind that the phone call may be just the tip of the iceberg, and what may seem like a fairly innocuous situation can quickly escalate.[25]

Other Risk Assessment Instruments and Tools

Other threat assessment tools and tests have been created as a means to systematically document and intervene in intimate partner violence cases. The Danger Assessment is one instrumental tool used to determine the chance of lethality or near-lethality in an intimate partner violence case, and it has already been discussed in this chapter. There are three other important risk assessment methods that could be used to minimize the risk of threat in these types of situations.

Table 7.1 is a chart describing the risk assessment methods outlined in Campbell's research (the Danger Assessment included).[26]

Illinois Dangerousness Assessment for Setting Bail

Summary of 725 ILCS 5/110–5.1

One of the most dangerous times for victims of domestic violence is the period between their attacker's arrest and his or her prosecution.[27] Many states have addressed this danger by enacting statutes imposing a presumption of conditional bail and a requirement to appear before a judge or magistrate for the setting of bail.[28] Illinois enacted such a statute in 2007 by amending the Code of Criminal Procedure of 1963.[29] Under 725 ILCS 5/110–5.1, "a person charged with committing a violence crime against a family or household member" is required to "appear before the court for the setting of bail if specified conditions are met."[30] Such a condition exists if the person charged, at the time of the alleged offense,

(1) Was subject to an order of protection or was convicted of a violation of an order of protection, and the victim was a family or household member at the time of the offense;

Table 7.1 outlines four popular methods of Risk Assessment and can be found in Jacquelyn Campbell's *Intimate Partner Violence Risk Assessment Validation Study, Final Report* (2005)

Description of Four Risk Assessment Methods

Method	Description	Administration	Primary intended uses
Danger Assessment (Campbell, 1986, 1995, 2003)	Review of past year with a calendar to document severity and frequency of battering and 20 yes/no questions about risk factors **Scoring:** −3 to 40 and four risk categories (variable, increased, severe, and extreme danger)	Interview with the victim, usually by victim advocate	Assess risk of extreme dangerousness and lethal violence for victim education, awareness, safety planning and service provision
DV-MOSAIC (Gavin de Becker and Associates, 2001)	Computer-assisted method that includes 46 multiple response items about risk and protective factors **Scoring:** program computes risk score of 1–10 and a missing data (IQ) score	Criminal justice professional enters responses after victim, perhaps offender, and other interviews; reviews of criminal records and police reports	Assess immediate, short-term threat of severe or lethal domestic violence situations for victim awareness, safety planning, further investigation, and criminal justice responses
Domestic Violence Screening Instrument (Williams and Houghton, 2004)	12 questions given 0–3 points, primarily related to offender's criminal history, employment, and several other risk factors **Scoring:** risk score 0–30, and two risk categories (not high risk and high risk)	Probation or other court officer completes instrument based on offender's criminal record and interview	Assess risk of recidivism/re-assault for supervision, probation/parole, and other offender-related decisions
Kingston Screening Instrument for Domestic Violence (Gelles, 1988)	10 questions about risk factors, each with 2 to 3 response categories, and an offender's poverty status scale **Scoring:** risk scores of 0 to 10 and four risk categories (low, moderate, high, or very high)	Offender and victim interviews and review of police reports by probation or other court officer	Assess risk of recidivism/re-assault for offender charging and supervision decisions, set conditions for release, probation, and protective orders
Victim Assessment of Risk (Goodman, Dutton and Bennett, 2000; Heckert and Gondolf, 2004; Weisz, Tolman and Saunders, 2000)	2 questions about victim's perception of the likelihood that she will be physically assaulted or seriously hurt by abuser in the next year **Scoring:** victim rates likelihood on a scale of 1–10		

(2) Was convicted of a violent crime and the victim was a family or household member at the time of the offense; or

(3) Was convicted of a violation of a substantially similar municipal ordinance or law of this or any state or the United States and the victim was a family or household member at the time of the offense.[31]

The aforementioned condition also exists if the arresting officer "observed on the alleged victim objective manifestations of physical harm" believed to be a result of the alleged offense, believes that the person possessed a deadly weapon at the time of the offense, or believes that the person presents a threat of serious physical harm to the alleged victim or to any other person if released on bail.[32]

The stature further requires a court to consider a set of factors when setting bail for a person charged with committing a violent crime against a family or household member and who is required to appear before the court for the setting of bail. These factors include:

(1) Whether the person has a history of domestic violence or a history of other violent acts;

(2) The mental health of the person;

(3) Whether the person has a history of violating the orders of any court or governmental entity;

(4) Whether the person is potentially a threat to any other person;

(5) Whether the person has access to deadly weapons or a history of using deadly weapons;

(6) Whether the person has a history of abusing alcohol or any controlled substance;

(7) The severity of the alleged violence that is the basis of the alleged offense, including, but not limited to, the duration of the alleged violent incident, and whether the alleged violent incident involved serious physical injury, sexual assault, strangulation, abuse during the alleged victim's pregnancy, abuse of pets, or forcible entry to gain access to the alleged victim;

(8) Whether a separation of the person from the alleged victim or a termination of the relationship between the person and the alleged victim has recently occurred or is pending;

(9) Whether the person has exhibited obsessive or controlling behaviors toward the alleged victim, including, but not limited to, stalking, surveillance, or isolation of the alleged victim;

(10) Whether the person has expressed suicidal or homicidal ideations;

(11) Any information contained in the complaint and any police reports, affidavits, or other documents accompanying the complaint.[33]

As of 2014, 22 states had enacted statutes similar to 725 ILCS 5/110–5.1, including Michigan, New York, Ohio, and Texas.[34] Many other states have also enacted different types of statutes regarding bail for those charged with domestic violence crimes. Five states have enacted provisions that call for denial of bail for those believed to have committed a domestic violence crime.[35] Seven states, meanwhile, have enacted statutes whereby the person who allegedly committed a domestic violence crime is not required to go before a judge or may avoid doing so if certain conditions are met.[36] In California, the defendant is not required to go before a judge if the "arresting officer determines there is not a reasonable likelihood that the offense will continue."[37] In states with these types of statutes, when the defendant is not required to appear before a judge, the police officer can set bail and also impose conditions upon release.[38]

Often times the assistant district attorney may not have the answers to the danger assessment available for the bail hearing. Therefore, it is critical that any individuals having regular contact with the victim obtain and file this information for future court hearings. The answers to these questions can make the difference as to whether or not a substantial bail will be set by the judge. Often times these offenders do not have a criminal background and expect a low or no bond in these types of cases. However, if the judge is able to obtain information regarding the abovementioned questions, they may determine that the offender is indeed a threat to the victim and the community, and make their decision for bail accordingly.

Conclusion

Risk assessment for domestic violence victims is absolutely critical to help predict how far along the former partner is on the path to violence. Most of the time, intimate partner abuse cases have a very predictable cycle and pattern. Most abusers, whether educated or uneducated, will use many of the same techniques to exert power and control over their former partner. Incorporating a questionnaire, or one of the lethality assessments discussed in this chapter, will serve to help protect not only the abused partner, but also everyone else who is in her vicinity. If it is determined that an individual is in a potentially abusive situation, whether or not they have separated from the abuser, it is recommended that you inform them of local and national domestic violence and/or stalking organizations. These not-for-profit organizations can provide the partner in danger with safety planning, shelters, and often legal assistance. Take the time to learn about the local, state, and national domestic violence resources. By having an understanding of the pre-incident indicators in these types of cases, and taking a proactive approach to gather this information for the risk assessment professionals or law enforcement, you have the power to save lives.

Notes

1 Originally published by the American Psychology Association, available at: CNN.com, www. cnn.com/2013/12/06/us/domestic-intimate-partner-violence-fast-facts/index.html; originally published by Centers for Disease Control and Prevention, available at: CNN.com; originally published by the American Psychology Association, available at: CNN.com; Kiesel, Diane, *Domestic Violence: Law Policy and Practice*, Newark, NJ: LexisNexis Matthew Bender, (2007), published by Safe Horizon, available at: www.safehorizon.org/page/domestic-violence-statistics-facts-52.html.
2 Lemon, Nancy K.D., *Domestic Violence Law*, St. Paul, MN: LEG, Inc. doing business as West Academic (2013).
3 Ibid., 37.
4 Mahoney, Martha, *Legal Images of Battered Women: Redefining the Issue of Separation*, Ann Arbor, MI: The Michigan Law Review Association (1991).
5 Dansie, Susan J., *Lethality Assessment and Safety Planning* (1992). Available at: www.ncdsv.org/images/LethalityAssessmentSafetyPlanning.pdf.
6 CDC/NIOSH, Violence. *Occupational Hazards in Hospitals* (2002).
7 ASIS Commission on Standards and Guidelines, *Workplace Violence Prevention and Intervention Standard* (2011).
8 Cynthia L. Bischof Memorial Foundation (2015). Available at: www.cindysmemorial.org.
9 Lansu, Michael, Nadia Ezaldein fatally shot in shooting at downtown Nordstrom, Chicago: *The Chicago Sun-times* (2014). Available at: http://homicides.suntimes.com/2014/11/30/nadia-ezaldein-fatally-shot-in-shooting-at-downtown-nordstrom/.
10 Roehl, Janice, O'Sullivan, Chris, Webster, Daniel, Campbell, Jacquelyn, *Intimate Partner Violence Risk Assessment Validation Study, Final Report*, published by Safe Horizon (2005), available at: www. safehorizon.org/page/domestic-violence-statistics-facts-52.html.
11 Ibid., *supra* note 9.
12 Campbell, Jacquelyn, Commentary on Websdale, lethality assessment approaches: Reflections on their use and ways forward, *Violence against Women*, 11, 9, 1214–1221 (2005). Available at: www. baylor.edu/content/services/document.php/28821.pdf.

13 Ibid.

14 Ibid., *supra* note 5.

15 Ibid., *supra* note 10. More information about the purpose and structure of the Danger Assessment is outlined on the website: www.dangerassessment.org.

16 Paziotopoulos, Pam, Runge, Robin, What employers can do to minimize the impact of domestic violence and stalking in the workplace (2008). This chapter was published in *Preventing and Managing Workplace Violence: Legal and Strategic Guidelines*, ed. Mark A. Lies, Chicago, IL: ABA Publishing, 258–290.

17 Ibid., *supra* note 10. Original research conducted by Daly, M., Wiseman, K.A., Wilson, M., Women with children sired by previous partners incur excess risk of uxoricide, *Homicide Studies*, 1, 1, 61–71 (1997).

18 See National Center for Victims of Crime, Stalking Resource Center, *Fact Sheet on Stalking*, available at: http://victimsofcrime.org/docs/default-source/src/stalking-fact-sheet-2015_eng.pdf?sfvrsn=2; Stalking Resource Center website: http://victimsofcrime.org/our-programs/stalking-resource-center.

19 Ibid.

20 Ibid.

21 Ibid., *supra* note 10.

22 Ibid. Original research conducted by Arbuckle, J., Olson, L., Howard, M., Brillman, J., Ancti, C., Sklar, D., Safe at home? Domestic violence and other homicides among women in Mexico, *Annals of Emergency Medicine*, 27, 2, 210–215 (1996).

23 Ibid.

24 Ibid.

25 Paziotopoulos, Pam, Domestic violence and the workplace, *Workplace Violence Prevention Book*, C TAB F, Specialty Technical Publishers Reference Guide, STP Publishers, chapter 1 (2002).

26 Ibid., *supra* note 10.

27 Wagage, Suraji R., When the consequences are life and death: Pretrial detention for domestic violence offenders, 7 *Drexel Law Review*, 195, 211 (2014).

28 Ibid., 212.

29 2006 Ill. Legis. Serv. P.A. 94–878 (H.B. 4649) (WEST) (eff. Jan. 1, 2007); 725 Ill. Comp. Stat. Ann. § 5/110–5.1 (West eff. Jan. 25, 2013).

30 IL H.R. B. Stat. 2005–2006 Reg. Sess. H.B. 4649.

31 725 Ill. Comp. Stat. Ann. § 5/110–5.1 (West eff. Jan. 25, 2013).

32 Ibid.

33 Ibid.

34 Wagage, *supra* note 27 at 216, FN 144.

35 Ibid., 216–217, 223. These states include Florida, Massachusetts, and New Hampshire.

36 Ibid., 217. These states include California, Louisiana, and Pennsylvania.

37 Ibid., Cal. Penal Code § 853.6 (West 2012).

38 Wagage, *supra* note 27 at 217.

8 Case Studies

One thing we have learned over the last 20 plus years of investigating, assessing, mitigating, and managing threatening behaviors, threats, and acts of violence is that "you can't make this stuff up!" In this chapter we will talk about strategies to investigate, assess, mitigate, and monitor incidents and threat management issues. What makes threat management so challenging is the fact that each case is unique and must be assessed and mitigated according to the facts and circumstances that are known at that time. Your assessment and mitigation plan can change when new information comes to light, and it is important to remember you are dealing with a snap shot in time. The uniqueness of each case is based on the fact that no two humans are alike, and thus human behavior expressed in similar circumstances will likely be different, so we base our assessments and strategies on the behaviors displayed at a particular time.

Case Example 1

Stalking cases can be very high-risk cases that consume a great deal of time and stretch your resources. Here is one example. A husband and wife working at the same company, at the same location, but in different buildings were going through relationship problems. The husband had been on a medical leave of absence for several months and had been verbally and mentally abusing the wife at home and through emails. The wife left the house to live with friends of whom the husband was unaware, and she filed for divorce. (As we know, when one of the parties in an abusive relationship terminates that relationship and/or leaves the house, this could cause an escalation of threatening behaviors or threats and increase the likelihood for violence to occur.) The husband became very upset and started calling the wife on her cell phone and her work phone, leaving threatening voice messages alleging that violence would happen to her and her pet unless she returned to the house. The wife, concerned for her safety, contacted security at her company for assistance.

Security assisted her in filing a police report regarding the threatening voice messages and provided her with a personal safety plan for both at work and when away from work. The husband was now leaving voice messages with his co-workers, threatening them and their families and causing them to fear for their safety. The husband had a blog and was posting information regarding the wife and her activities. Security worked with local law enforcement, and several police reports were filed regarding the threatening voice messages. Security, human resources, and the employee assistance program (EAP) met with the husband's co-workers to discuss the company's response to the threats and provide them with resources. Security worked with company attorneys and law enforcement for 25 days and filed over 70 misdemeanor and two felony counts with the district attorney's office against the husband.

The judge in the case did not agree with the district attorney in the filing of numerous charges against the husband and combined the case into two misdemeanor counts of harassment. The wife provided the company with evidence that the husband was attempting to purchase a 45 caliber hand gun and had discovered where the wife was living. The company was able to obtain a corporate restraining order against the husband and decided to terminate his employment based on his threatening behaviors and threats. The wife also obtained a restraining order against the husband. The company used physical surveillance to monitor the husband prior to and after his notification of termination, which was done via registered US Mail to keep him from coming back to the workplace. One week after the corporate restraining order was served, the husband was arrested for violation of both restraining orders and was arrested again the following week for again violating the orders. After the second arrest, the husband stopped contacting the company.

In this case, several strategies were deployed to keep the workplace safe and the wife safe while she was at work. Security had issued a Be On the Look Out (BOLO) bulletin for the security officers and the lobby receptionist at the entrance points to the site that provided a physical description, a photo of the suspect, a brief summary of why the husband was not allowed in the workplace, and instructions on what to do if he showed up at the site. You can also take a copy of the BOLO and have each officer and lobby receptionist read the BOLO and sign the back showing they have read it as a way to ensure the officer or lobby receptionist is aware of the issue. This was done in case the husband attempted to enter the workplace to gain access to the wife or his former co-workers. The company was able to obtain a corporate restraining order against the husband, and this allowed the company to work with law enforcement each time the court order was violated and to arrest him; after the second arrest, this eventually persuaded the husband to stop the threatening communications with the company.

> **TIP:** *In each case you should evaluate the situation and information to see whether a restraining order is an option to use in the case you are dealing with. Depending on the case, a restraining order may or may not be a useful option. You will have to evaluate the situation based on the suspect's past and current behaviors and level of risk. Then, consult with your legal counsel and law enforcement. It is important to understand the restraining/protective order process in your state and whether your state has a corporate restraining order.*

The use of a physical surveillance provider can provide real-time valuable information for your threat management team (TMT) on the subject's activities and behaviors when they are away from the workplace. You may find that the subject is acquiring weapons or ammunition or is frequenting a shooting range. The subject may be giving away or selling items he or she may value. You may find that the subject is driving toward or has made several attempts to approach the workplace. In one high-risk case we worked on, the subject was seen buying street drugs in a park. In another case, the subject was loading weapons and ammunition into his vehicle and driving at high speed toward the workplace. The use of surveillance can also show that the subject is going on with their life and filing for unemployment or seeking new employment.

Surveillance can be very costly, depending on how long the coverage is needed, and having an experienced and reliable surveillance provider who knows the state laws that govern their operations is very important. Surveillance can be very difficult and requires an experienced team to provide useful and timely information to the client. Meeting with your surveillance provider and setting out your expectations and requirements is also very important. You should require your provider to contact the local law enforcement agency to advise them of the surveillance detail and whom they are watching and why. This will help to avoid any confusion or compromise to the surveillance activities that might arise if neighbors or someone else reports a suspicious vehicle or subject in the area.

Provide the surveillance team with a photo and a physical description of the subject they will be watching, including any vehicles they own and the address of their residence. Supply the team with information on whom the subject might target, including a photo, the address where they are living, and the type of vehicle they drive. This will make the team aware if the subject is in an area where one of his targets lives. The team will need to know specific information on the subject's threatening behaviors and threats that he or she might have made. Does the subject own or have access to any weapons? Does the subject have any former military or law enforcement training? Has there been any prior corrective action by the company, or does the subject have a criminal history, including past arrests and a history of violent behavior, that may suggest a propensity to future violence?

Case Example 2

Kim and Jim worked on the same floor of an office building. They worked in different departments and did not know each other. Jim would walk by Kim and make comments such as "it's red sweater day" or "it's brown shoe day." Kim did not know Jim and did not pay much attention to what he said as he walked by her. One day Kim was at the grocery store and saw Jim in the parking lot, and he waved at her. Another day when she was at home working in the front yard, Jim drove by, waved, and said hi. Kim just figured he must live in the area and it was coincidental that she saw him.

One evening when Kim was at home, someone knocked on her front door. Kim's husband answered the door, and it was Jim. Jim told the husband that Kim had sent him a text message to come over to the house. The husband had Kim come to the front door, and in the meantime, Jim left. The next day a neighbor told Kim and her husband that someone fitting the description of Jim was sitting in a car watching their house. Kim and her husband were concerned, and Kim contacted security at her work and told them what was going on. Kim provided a statement to security and human resources detailing the suspicious activities involving Jim that took place away from the workplace. The only workplace-related incidents that Kim knew about were the comments Jim had made about what clothing items she was wearing, and to her knowledge she had no other contact with Jim at work.

With most of the stalking activity taking place away from the workplace, the company was limited in how it could respond. Security advised Kim on the process for obtaining a restraining order and advised her to report the incidents to the law enforcement agency in her city. Kim filed a police report and was granted a temporary restraining order against Jim. Kim provided a copy of the order to security and human resources. One evening after Jim was served with the restraining order, he was seen by a neighbor looking through a window at Kim's residence and fled when the neighbor yelled at him. The police responded, but Jim had fled the area.

Kim reported this to her company, and the TMT convened and decided that Jim should be interviewed about the restraining order and advised to stay away from Kim at work. Security went to interview Jim, and he became belligerent, left the interview, returned to his office, packed his personal belongings, and retired on the spot. Security contacted the detective who was handling Kim's case and advised them of Jim's behavior. The detective interviewed Jim and let him know he would be arrested if he violated the restraining order; this stopped Jim's stalking behaviors toward Kim, as far as she knew.

The difficulty with this case is that the stalking behaviors were taking place away from work, and the actions the company could take were limited. The plan the TMT came up with was to interview him about the restraining order and issue him with an expected workplace conduct notice acknowledgement, but he refused to cooperate during the interview and retired from the company. The expected workplace conduct notice acknowledgement would have advised Jim on his expected conduct while at work, and if he violated the provisions laid out in the notice, he would receive corrective action, up to and including discharge. The expected workplace conduct notice acknowledgement can be used when there is a restraining or protective order in place or when it is needed to deal with an issue between two employees. In the notice you can stipulate what building or floor they will not be allowed in, where they can park their vehicle, what entrance to use, or even what bathroom in the building to use.

The notice should be given to both Jim and Kim to make sure they understand that the notice applies to each of them and will be in place as long as the company decides it is needed. This might upset the victim, in this case Kim, and make her feel as if she is being victimized again, and it should be explained to her that she and Jim must abide by the agreement. In some cases when we have used a workplace conduct notice acknowledgement, the victim has violated the restraining order or the notice, so both parties must understand they have to follow the stipulations in the notice or face corrective action. In all cases, we must ensure that the entire workforce is safe. As we mentioned, stalking cases can be time consuming, can draw on your resources, and can escalate very quickly into a high-risk or life-threatening situation. A stalking case can also be very frustrating when the victim is not willing to take the steps to help protect themselves or their family. There is only so much security and law enforcement can do, and we can never guarantee the victim's safety or that the suspect will stop the stalking behavior. With stalking and domestic violence cases, the suspect knows they can find the victim at their place of work at least five days a week, and this makes the workplace vulnerable to a potential incident of threatening behavior, threats, or an act of violence.

In Chapter 3 of this book we discussed the importance of categorizing threat management incidents. We have assault and battery as two of the categories for a specific reason. We like to know, when an incident actually involves one employee touching another employee, whether it is a poke, a push, a punch, or striking with a mechanism. An assault would be an incident whereby the suspect had the present ability to batter the victim and stopped prior to any physical contact taking place, or an attempt to strike someone that failed (e.g., swinging at someone and missing, or throwing an object at someone and missing).

Case Example 3

A manager was having his team clean up their area for an upcoming quality inspection and asked his employee Bob to clean up his area for the inspection. The manager knew Bob had an issue with his temper and did not get along with his co-workers, so the manager volunteered to assist Bob. The manager approached Bob and told him he would help him with the cleanup, which enraged Bob. He started throwing items around the area, swearing at the manager, and telling him to get out of his area. The manager attempted to explain to Bob why they needed to clean up the area, and Bob started swinging and chasing the manager with the broom. The manager, fearing for his safety, fled the area and called security.

The manager had a reasonable expectation that he would have been struck with the broom if he had not fled from Bob. The threat in this case was Bob's attempt to get his manager to leave the area by a show of force while swinging the broom and chasing his manager with it or to inflict injury on his manager, and Bob had the apparent and present ability to carry out the threat. The employee did not have to tell the manager he was going to hit him with the broom; the combination of swinging the broom and chasing the manager constituted the act of an assault.

Looking at this case from an investigative standpoint, one thing we want to caution you on are the questions you ask the victim: in this case, the manager. Asking the manager if Bob had threatened him might not be the right question. Bob was swearing and yelling at the manager but made no verbal threat toward him. So if the manager is asked whether Bob threatened him, the answer might be no. This case might not be categorized or investigated as a threat management or even a possible criminal incident. Obviously the manager felt threatened, or he would not have fled the area or called security. Questions you might want to ask, whether it be in this case or in any other threat case, are "Did you feel threatened?" and "Why did you feel threatened?". You want to understand from the victim why they felt in fear for their safety and ask them to explain so that you can understand from their perspective why this was a threat to them. In this case, knowing that Bob had had prior corrective actions related to his temper and threatening behaviors helped the TMT in their assessment of the risk Bob posed to the workplace. By piecing together the past history and the current incident, the TMT could better understand the future behavior Bob might exhibit if he was allowed to return to the workplace.

Case Example 4

In this example of an assault case, we talk about the challenges of working threat management issues internationally, where customs and cultures can influence someone's behaviors and where law and regulations are very different from those in the United States, Canada, or the United Kingdom.

John worked in a large manufacturing facility in Asia, and was the manager of a group until his job performance became poor and abnormal behavior caused him to be removed from his management position and placed in a role where he was working in a cubicle by himself. John was a contract employee and, like most of the workers, was on a year-by-year contract. Due to his poor job performance, the company notified him that his contract would not be renewed and he would have to find employment elsewhere. This angered John, and he started sending email messages to his manager, Tim, which increased in frequency and then became threatening. John was blaming Tim for his problems at work and telling him he would not be able to provide for his family without his job. John became more disruptive at work toward the end of his contract and was put on paid leave until his contract expired.

One day, John's wife and mother came to the main lobby at the office complex and demanded to see Tim. When Tim tried to talk with the two ladies, they became upset and started vandalizing the lobby, crying and refusing to leave the building until the local police arrived and asked them to leave.

John was seen hanging around the facility during shift change and continued to send emails to company executives demanding that his job be reinstated and making conditional threats if it was not. The general manager (GM) for the facility reported that John had tried to gain entry to his gated neighborhood and had been stopped by the security officer twice in one week. At one point, John had gained access into the GM's gated neighborhood and was seen outside the GM's house. The international TMT had been involved in this case for three months by this time and had suggested increasing the security at the GM's house and at the site. The company had arranged for one of its security managers in the region to go to the site to conduct an assessment of the GM's house and the facility.

Prior to the security assessment, one morning John had gained access to the facility using a fake contractor's badge and had two meat cleavers in his possession. John went to Tim's office, but he was not there. John proceeded to hack up Tim's desk with one of the meat cleavers and left it stuck in the wooden desk. John then headed to the GM's office and on his way ran into Tim. He grabbed Tim, pinned him against a wall, and started yelling at him, holding the second meat cleaver close to Tim's throat while making slashing motions with the meat cleaver. The GM heard the commotion and stepped out of his office to see what was going on. John saw the GM and chased after him. The GM and the others in the office were able to run into a conference room and lock the door so John could not enter. Security and local police were called; however, John was able to leave the area before the police arrived.

The company had security cameras in the building. One captured John's assault on Tim, and the video was shown to the local police. Since John was gone and no one was physically injured, the local police refused to take any action. The TMT contacted the Regional Security Office at the US Embassy and asked for assistance in working with the local police for support in this case.

TIP: *Companies should consider having an international TMT that is country or regionally based, comprised of security, human resources, legal, and employee assistance program. In this case, the company had an in-country law firm that supported the company on in-country issues. They were brought into the TMT meetings to give guidance on the laws and regulations of the country and assisted in mitigating the issue. Through the in-country law firm, a local security company conducted an assessment and identified what additional security measures were needed for the GM and his family and residence. It is always important to have in-country contacts that can provide legal and security resources when needed. Being able to establish these contacts before you need them is very valuable when doing business internationally.*

Working with the Regional Security Office at the US Embassy, a liaison was established with the local police, and the in-country law firm representing the company started working with the local police to deal with the threat that John posed to the company and its employees. It was discovered that John's father was a retired chief of detectives for the local police, and this might have caused some hesitation in the response from the local police for support. It also appeared that the local police were aware that John might have some mental health issues. One of the options was to have John evaluated for his mental health issues by the Country Medical Office. In the country concerned, if John was diagnosed as having a mental health problem he would be deemed non-employable, and his family would be responsible for taking care of him for the rest of his life. It was decided to meet with John's father and the local police to work on a plan to have the father and the family seek medical help for John in dealing with his mental health problems. From this point on, John would only communicate with the company through his father. As part of the company's "soft landing" approach, a nine-month severance package for John was provided, with the condition that it would be revoked if John made contact or acted out against the company or its employees in any manner. John ceased his communications with the company and has been complying with the separation agreement.

Dealing with threat management issues internationally is very challenging for a company. It is important to have resources established strategically across the globe that can support your operations and offices in a timely manner. This will help to mitigate risk and keep your employees safe while working within the laws and regulations, and understanding the customs, of that country. Your threat management procedure should be written so that it applies to the entire company (at domestic and non-U.S. locations), with requirements that address any variance based on international laws and regulations.

Case Example 5

The threat management category Abnormal Behavior is defined as behavior that causes discomfort to others, deviation from typical patterns and actions, and demonstration of emotions of concern. This can be the person who is wearing an aluminum foil hat and telling his co-workers that the hat keeps the electronic waves from affecting his brain, or the female co-worker who is seen talking to the parts on her workbench and, when asked by her manager why she is talking to the parts, responds by telling the manager that the parts are talking back to her. Many times these abnormal behaviors cause co-workers concern for their safety and concern that the subject may act out in a violent manner, which causes disruption in the workgroup. These can be tough issues for managers and co-workers to deal with. It has been our experience that when these issues are left unattended or ignored, these behaviors can escalate and result in a serious or life-threatening event.

Jason sits in a cubicle area with his other co-workers, is quiet, and keeps to himself. One day he mentions to a co-worker that he is concerned about his wife and thinks she might be an alien, and the co-worker laughs it off. Over the next few weeks, Jason approaches others in the workgroup and talks about his belief that his wife is an alien. He tells them she used to have a scar on her back and now it is gone. Jason starts to talk every day about his wife and the strange things she is doing that substantiate his belief. Jason's obsession and constant conversations about this are affecting his productivity and making the workgroup feel uncomfortable around him and concerned for their safety. Until a few weeks ago, Jason had been a good performer at work and had no issues. His manager is concerned for Jason and the workgroup and contacts human resources and the EAP for guidance. It is decided that due to the decline in his work performance, they will mandate a fitness for duty EAP evaluation. Jason complies with the request and meets with EAP. Jason is on leave for a few months while his condition is being treated and is cleared to return to work. When Jason's manager is informed that he is cleared to return, the manager tells human resources he doesn't want Jason back in the workgroup because he feels Jason is crazy. The TMT meets with his manager and develops a plan for Jason's return to the workgroup. The manager is advised that if Jason starts to exhibit the same behaviors, EAP should be notified right away and Jason should be talked to about his disruptive behavior.

There are people in the workplace who have mental health issues and take medication to help them deal with their medical issues. We see from time to time that when these folks stop taking their medication, these abnormal or threatening behaviors may return and cause problems in the workplace. We as TMTs are responsible for dealing with the threatening behaviors and must take action based on the behaviors and actions of the individual. It is ultimately up to the employee to take their medication. However, they are still responsible for their behavior—they are not allowed to act out and threaten anyone. There are consequences that come with their actions.

In another situation, Dale contacts the security manager at his workplace and asks him if security is following him. The manager replies "no." Dale tells the manager that he believes the Government is following him around town and has put agents in the attic of his apartment to watch him at night. He explains how he is sleeping on the floor so they cannot see him at night and that they are taking pictures of him when he is at the beach. Dale spends the next hour giving details about how he is being followed and asking the manager to have the Government stop the surveillance. The manager contacts the TMT and asks for their assistance. Dale's manager tells the team that Dale is a good worker and has never exhibited any abnormal behavior in the workplace prior to this incident.

The security manager and Dale's human resources representative meet with him, and he tells them his belief about the Government following him. They ask Dale if he would like to meet with the EAP counselor, and he refuses, saying he is not crazy. Dale resigned from the company the next day. When dealing with some of these issues, there is only so much we can do as TMTs, and we have to understand that if the person is not willing to seek assistance in dealing with their issue, we cannot force them. Dale committed suicide two weeks after he resigned.

Case Example 6

In the workplace, communicated threat cases are very common. When we look at communicated threats, we are talking about an expression of an intention to injure another person. This can be done verbally, in writing, by gesture, or by electronic means. There is the indirect or veiled threat, which is not specific, such as "Let's take this outside" or "We can finish this after work." The threat is implying that some type of action will take place if they go outside, and this is how the person being threatened perceives the threat.

Blackmail is a good example of a conditional threat. For instance, an individual can threaten another individual by telling them that if they do not do something, for example, buy them lunch, "I will tell our manager about you taking a long break," or in a more threatening vein, "If you touch my stuff again, I will break your nose."

A direct threat is straightforward and leaves no room for misunderstanding on the part of the targeted person. It offers no exemptions, options, or conditions. The threat message is often simple, direct, and sincere, such as "I will punch you in the face."

The key here is what the threatener intended or meant by it, and the best way to find that out is to ask them. We have heard comments from managers that "Oh, he didn't mean it, he was just blowing off steam" or "They were just joking around." When we are assessing threats, we need to know what the threatener meant when they made the threat, and whether they have the means and wherewithal to carry out the threat. An expression can still be viewed as threatening even if it is determined that the threatener has no intention of actually carrying it out, if the person reasonably believes it is a threat and is in fear for his or her own safety or the safety of others. As threat assessors, we need to ask those questions that will help us better understand the threat and the past history that led up to the threat being made. This will allow us to ascertain the possibility of some type of future violence occurring.

The category of Battery is defined as intentionally or recklessly causing physical contact or bodily harm performed against another without their consent. This can be with hands, body, or a mechanism. Most of the time, battery cases are clear-cut issues for organizations to deal with. Employee A hit employee B in the face with a closed fist. For many companies, this means an instant termination of employment. As threat assessors, we want to know why employee A hit employee B, what circumstances led up to this attack, and whether there are other issues we need to deal with. Could employee A continue his targeting of employee B or the workplace after the termination? Could employee A return to the facility and retaliate against the company for his termination and the way he perceived he was treated while he was an employee? If we are going to terminate employee A, we might be dealing with a hostile termination and should set up a plan to safely carry out the termination.

In this chapter, we have given case examples of threat management incidents and provided some guidance on how to identify, assess, respond to, mitigate, and monitor these cases. An important point is to always follow up or investigate allegations or concerns brought forward to your organization to make sure they are looked at thoroughly. Threatening behaviors and threats that go unaddressed or ignored can be very costly for a company or organization. If violence occurs as a result of these unaddressed behaviors, the result could be serious bodily injury or death as well as millions of dollars in damages from lawsuits, damaged reputation, and lost productivity. It is easier to explain why we took the actions we did based on our training and experience than to attempt to explain why we failed to take any action.

9 Research in Assessing Levels of Threat

Implications for Workplace Violence Training

Marizen Ramirez, Corinne Peek-Asa, and Carri Casteel

Introduction

Each year in the United States, more than 700 workers are killed (Bureau of Labor Statistics, 2015) and nearly 7 million experience a nonfatal assault while at work (Schat et al., 2006). Nearly 30% of U.S. workplaces experiencing a violent event report heightened fear among employees, decreased morale and productivity, and higher turnover (Bureau of Labor Statistics, 2006). Workplace violence is repeatedly reported by businesses as a leading security threat (Securitas, 2015), and it is estimated that millions of dollars are spent each year on lost productivity, medical claims, and litigation.

Most acts of violence do not occur without warning. As mentioned in a previous chapter of this book and in several forensic analyses of extreme cases of workplace violence, perpetrators exhibit premeditated behaviors such as selecting targets, purchasing weapons, and communicating plans to others (Meloy et al., 2012; Calhoun and Weston, 2003; Borum et al., 1999; Fein et al., 1995). In other cases, acts of aggression begin with verbal threats and harassment that escalate in frequency and severity over time. Monitoring and managing threats of violence, or threat assessment, are critical functions in a comprehensive workplace violence prevention program (ASIS/SHRM, 2011; Kenny, 2010; Chauhan, 1999; Clements et al., 2005).

A variety of employees may engage in threat assessment. At the level of the work unit, managers must immediately assess potential threats encountered among their unit staff. As additional resources and support are required, threats might be brought to the attention of departmental units such as human resources or security, and in more extreme and complex cases, the top levels of an organization. Threat assessment is also a key task of threat management teams (TMTs) (ASIS/SHRM, 2011; Kenny, 2010). TMTs are multi-disciplinary teams that function at a higher level of an organization and draw on expertise from various departments such as security, human resources, legal, and medical to identify potential threats of violence and to develop mitigation strategies (ASIS/SHRM, 2011).

Effective threat assessment requires specialized training (Wade, 2004) to optimize identification of and response to potential threats, especially since a comprehensive approach goes beyond recognizing threats or warning signs of violence (Howard, 2001). Threat assessment involves critical thinking and a working understanding of threat level severities that might be defined in company policies or provided through formal training. Methods for training in threat assessment vary from lecture-based education training (McNiel et al., 2008) to the use of vignettes (Storey et al., 2011) or clinical examples (Reynolds and Miles, 2009). Evaluations of the effectiveness of these methods have been conducted to a limited extent. A one-hour violence risk assessment training of mental health professionals improved risk assessment skills (McNiel et al., 2008), and an eight-day, 54-hour course increased the knowledge, skills, and confidence of criminal justice professionals in conducting violence risk assessments (Storey et al., 2011). However, no studies have specifically focused on members of TMTs.

Simulation training is another method with great potential for training in threat assessment. In tabletop exercises, originally developed for disaster response, individuals are presented with a series of scenes from a hypothetical threat and asked to make response decisions at various time points (FEMA, 2015). Like disasters, workplace violence, especially in the most severe forms, is a relatively rare occurrence. Tabletop exercises provide an opportunity for many individuals to practice quick decision making by assessing realistic but hypothetical threats and developing response strategies. Tabletop exercises can also function as an evaluation tool for assessing baseline skills in threat assessment and understanding the critical thinking of participants. To our knowledge, only one study has reported the use of simulation training in the workplace through "structured improvisation workshops" to simulate a crisis and management strategies; however, its effectiveness was not assessed (Callahan, 1986).

The remainder of this chapter presents the results of a research study demonstrating the use of tabletop exercises to assess TMT member skills in threat assessment and their confidence in performing TMT responsibilities following tabletop exercise training.

Research Study

A total of 164 employees from a large multinational company participated in five company regional trainings. Individuals represented various departments within the company, including security and fire protection, human resources, corporate investigations, employee assistance programs, ethics, health services/medical, and legal. The employees were members of 22 TMTs from various locations throughout the United States with differing levels of experience in threat management. The level of experience of the TMT was determined through consultation with the company about each TMT's caseload and date of initiation; teams with high caseloads were considered more experienced, while teams with low caseloads were considered less experienced.

Tabletop Scenario Exercise

The research team developed two tabletop scenarios—one focused on workplace bullying and another on stalking in the workplace—based on prior investigations completed by the company as well as written company policies on threat assessment. This chapter reports on the findings from the bullying scenario. The scenarios included specific descriptions of behaviors consistent with threat levels defined by the company. For example, the bullying scenario included a description of verbal and physical intimidation as well as blocking behavior, which are indicators described in company guidelines to be consistent with a medium threat level. Scenarios were written in a format in which events unfolded in a step-wise fashion, and participants were asked to provide assessments, next actions, and rationale for each step at various time points. For each scenario, an initial scene was presented with minimal information, and participants were asked to individually assess the threat level (without input from other team members). As the scenario progressed with subsequent actions and information, team members collaborated on assessment and management. For this chapter, we focus on the individual assessments of threat to understand individual skills and familiarity with company guidelines.

Data Collection and Measures

To begin the bullying scenario, the moderator presented a situation in which the following anonymous letter had been received by human resources:

To Whom It May Concern:

   We have a situation that makes it very hard to work. Our boss, Mr. Sims has a "favorite" employee, and this guy really is a case. His name is John Andrews. He bosses people around, gets in our faces, and can be a real aggressive jerk. Our boss asks this guy to take care of his work for him, like when the line is down he wants this guy to fix it instead of him. Well, he fixes it but in a really bad way, and when we complain he yells at us, threatens us, and then tells the boss that *we* are the problem. The boss doesn't do anything because he likes this guy. At least one guy, Ken Egan, complained to the boss, and now he's afraid the boss and this guy John Andrews have it in for him. On three occasions, I've seen Andrews blow up in Egan's face, and it's getting worse. Andrews intimidates and bullies us sometimes, especially Egan. The last time, Andrews blocked Egan from his work station because he thought Egan's break was too long—looked like they were going to duke it out. It's getting real bad down here so I thought I should say something. I'm not signing this because I'm worried they'll have it in for me, too.

After presentation of the initial scene, participants were provided with a semi-structured data collection instrument to answer the following questions about the incident:

1. *Threat level.* Individuals were asked to first assign the threat level for the scenario: low, medium, high, or unsure. Based on company threat assessment guidelines that provide a framework for assigning threat levels, this would represent a medium threat level. Individual threat levels were categorized as under-assess (a response of low threat), appropriate (a response of medium threat), over-assess (a response of high threat), or unsure.
2. *Reasons for threat level assignment.* Individuals were then asked to describe their reasons for their threat level assignment, which were used to determine whether company definitions and policies were used by individuals to guide their threat level decision. Two members of the research team independently coded open-ended responses and reached consensus through discussions. The following categories were used to code responses: presence of threat to physical safety/verbal intimidation was stated in the letter; letter included only limited information; status of the threat is unclear; behavioral history is mentioned; management and work unit issues are mentioned; specific reference to using company guidelines to guide decisions; other; and no answer.
3. *Documents used to define threat level.* Participants were then asked to identify which company guidelines or policies were used to assign threat levels. Participant responses were categorized as correct policy identified; incorrect policy identified; policy not specified; other; or no answer.
4. *Response steps.* After the assessment of the threat, participants were asked a series of questions about the next steps of engagement. Specifically, they were asked whether the threat should be investigated (yes, no, or don't know) and whether the TMT should be contacted about the incident (yes, no, or don't know). Participants then described, in an open-ended format, the reasons for contacting the TMT lead. Using the same process for coding reasons for threat level assignment, responses were coded into the following categories: TMT lead should be notified; TMT lead can provide assistance; company policy; reported physical confrontation; no physical violence; unknown extent of threats; and other.

Analysis

Percentages were used to examine the distribution of responses for the assignment of the level of threat, reasons for threat level assignment, and documents to define threat levels, overall and by participants' departments and experience. Similar descriptive statistics (percentages and frequencies) were used to describe the recommended steps of engagement (investigation, contact with the TMT) and reasons for contacting the TMT, by level of threat assignment.

Results

Threat Level Assessments

Of the total participants, 37% (n=61) assigned the level of threat (medium threat level) to the scenario according to company definitions and guidelines (Table 9.1). About 18% (n=29) under-assessed the threat level, 19% (n=31) over-assessed the threat level, and 26% (n=43) were unsure. There were no substantive differences by experience level of the team members. Slightly more individuals coming from the experienced than from the less experienced teams tended to under-assess the threat (20% vs. 15%). However, a slightly greater proportion (29%) from less experienced teams tended to be unsure of the threat level compared with those from more experienced teams (23%). Participants from security and corporate investigations and human resources departments had the most accurate assessments, with almost 40% appropriately assigning the threat level. EAP and health services had the greatest proportion of under-assessments (24%) and unsure assessments (34%).

Among those who appropriately assessed the level of threat, the most common reasons for their assignment were based on the anonymous letter's "threat to physical safety" (35%) and "behavioral history" (23%) (Table 9.2). These are both elements in the company's definition of a medium threat. Among those who under-assessed the threat, the most cited reasons for their assignment were the "lack of clarity about the physical nature of the threat" (36%) and "limited information or more investigation needed" (27%). And, among those who over-assessed the threat level, the most common reason for their assignment was the "threat to physical safety" (42%). "Work unit issues such as poor management or product failure" were cited as a reason among 13% overall but among 24% in the over-assessment group. Interestingly, only 28%–39% of all participants correctly identified the correct company policy that defines threat levels.

The thought process for the threat level assignment did not differ much by department (Table 9.3). "Physical threat" was the most common reason for the threat assignment overall (29%), but slightly more so for security and corporate investigations (31%) compared with human resources (25%) and EAP/health services (26%). Notably, however, EAP was most familiar with company guidelines, and about 44% cited the correct company document.

Table 9.1 Initial threat assessment, overall and by department

	Under	Appropriate	Over	Unsure	Total
	N (%)	*N (%)*	*N (%)*	*N (%)*	*N (%)*
Overall	29 (17.7)	61 (37.2)	31 (18.9)	43 (26.2)	164 (100.0)
Experience of site					
Less	12 (15.4)	28 (35.9)	15 (19.2)	23 (29.5)	78 (47.6)
More	17 (19.8)	33 (38.4)	16 (18.6)	20 (23.3)	86 (52.4)
TMT department					
Security/corporate investigations	13 (15.9)	31 (37.8)	18 (22.0)	20 (24.4)	82 (50.0)
Human resources	7 (17.1)	16 (39.0)	7 (17.1)	11 (26.8)	41 (25.0)
EAP/health services	7 (24.1)	8 (27.6)	4 (13.8)	10 (34.5)	29 (17.7)
Other	2 (16.7)	6 (50.0)	2 (16.7)	2 (16.7)	12 (7.3)

Table 9.2 Threat assessment decision process, by threat level

	Assessment of threat				
	Under	Appropriate	Over	Unsure	Total
	N (%)	N (%)	N (%)	N (%)	N (%)
Reason for threat level (N=261)					
Threat to physical safety/verbal intimidation/bullying/blocking	6 (13.6)	34 (35.1)	23 (41.8)	13 (20.0)	76 (29.1)
Limited information/more investigation needed/vague letter	12 (27.3)	12 (12.4)	2 (3.6)	22 (33.8)	48 (18.4)
Unclear threat/threat not clearly physical	16 (36.4)	15 (15.5)	1 (1.8)	15 (23.1)	47 (18.0)
Behavioral history/numerous occasions/escalation	2 (4.5)	22 (22.7)	14 (25.5)	4 (6.2)	42 (16.1)
Work unit issues/product failure/ poor management	5 (11.4)	11 (11.3)	13 (23.6)	6 (9.2)	35 (13.4)
Company guidelines	0 (0.0)	1 (1.0)	1 (1.8)	0 (0.0)	2 (0.8)
Other	3 (6.8)	2 (2.1)	1 (1.8)	3 (4.6)	9 (3.4)
No answer	0 (0.0)	0 (0.0)	0 (0.0)	2 (3.1)	2 (0.8)
Documents used to define threat level (N=190)					
Correct documentation used to assess threat level	14 (38.9)	19 (27.5)	10 (27.8)	19 (38.8)	62 (32.6)
Insufficient documentation used to assess threat level	13 (36.1)	22 (31.9)	12 (33.3)	16 (32.7)	63 (33.2)
Document not specified	1 (2.8)	7 (10.1)	3 (8.3)	3 (6.1)	14 (7.4)
Other	4 (11.1)	4 (5.8)	4 (11.1)	5 (10.2)	17 (8.9)
No answer	4 (11.1)	17 (24.6)	7 (19.4)	6 (12.2)	34 (17.9)

Participants also did not offer different reasons for their threat assignment according to the experience level of their TMT. The only notable difference is that less experienced teams cited "limited information/more investigation needed" as the reason for their threat assignment. Regardless of experience level, about a third of the participants identified the correct company policy for assigning threat levels.

Response Actions

Most participants recommended investigation as a next immediate step, including over 90% of those who appropriately or over-assessed the threat level, 79% of those who under-assessed, and 77% of those who were unsure of the threat level (Table 9.4). With the exception of the over-assessors, fewer participants recommended engaging the TMT at this point. All but one of the over-assessors recommended contacting the TMT lead compared with 64% of those who appropriately assigned the level of threat, 55% of those under-assessing the threat level, and 67% of those who were unsure. The most common reasons for contacting the TMT included that "the lead should be notified of potential threats or investigation steps," especially among those who over-assessed the threat (46%) but even among those who under-assessed the threat (39%) or were unsure (29%). The TMT was cited as a "source of assistance and instruction" by about 20% of participants overall, and particularly so among the over-assessors (36%) but not so commonly among under-assessors (9%). Another common reason was the

Table 9.3 Threat assessment decision process, by TMT department and site level of experience

	TMT department					Experience level		
	Security/ corporate investigations	Human resources	EAP/health services	Other*	Total	More	Less	Total
	N (%)	N (%)	N (%)	N(%)	N (%)	N (%)	N (%)	N (%)
Reason for threat level (N=261)								
Threat to physical safety/verbal intimidation/ bullying/blocking	39 (31.0)	16 (24.6)	13 (26.0)	8 (40.0)	76 (29.1)	41 (44.6)	35 (37.6)	76 (41.1)
Limited information/more investigation needed/ vague letter	23 (18.3)	15 (23.1)	8 (16.0)	2 (10.0)	48 (18.4)	21 (22.8)	27 (29.0)	48 (25.9)
Unclear threat/threat not clearly physical	21 (16.7)	9 (13.8)	12 (24.0)	5 (25.0)	47 (18.0)	23 (25.0)	24 (25.8)	47 (25.4)
Behavioral history/numerous occasions/ escalation	16 (12.7)	12 (18.5)	10 (20.0)	4 (20.0)	42 (16.1)	26 (28.3)	16 (17.2)	42 (22.7)
Work unit issues/product failure/poor management	19 (15.1)	9 (13.8)	6 (12.0)	1 (5.0)	35 (13.4)	17 (18.5)	18 (19.4)	35 (18.9)
Company guidelines	1 (0.8)	0 (0.0)	1 (2.0)	0 (0.0)	2 (0.8)	1 (1.1)	1 (1.1)	2 (1.1)
Other	6 (4.8)	3 (4.6)	0 (0.0)	0 (0.0)	9 (3.4)	4 (4.3)	5 (5.4)	9 (4.9)
No answer	1 (0.8)	1 (1.5)	0 (0.0)	0 (0.0)	2 (0.8)	0 (0.0)	2 (2.2)	2 (1.1)
Documents used to define threat level (N=190)								
Correct documentation used to assess threat level	28 (29.5)	18 (35.3)	14 (43.8)	2 (16.7)	62 (32.6)	31 (31.3)	31 (34.1)	62 (32.6)
Insufficient documentation used to assess threat level	29 (30.5)	21 (41.2)	8 (25.0)	5 (41.7)	63 (33.2)	31 (31.3)	32 (35.2)	63 (33.2)
Document not specified	6 (6.3)	2 (3.9)	5 (15.6)	1 (8.3)	14 (7.4)	12 (12.1)	2 (2.2)	14 (7.4)
Other	9 (9.5)	3 (5.9)	5 (15.6)	0 (0.0)	17 (8.9)	10 (10.1)	7 (7.7)	17 (8.9)
No answer	23 (24.2)	7 (13.7)	0 (0.0)	4 (33.3)	34 (17.9)	15 (15.2)	19 (20.9)	34 (17.9)

* Includes ethics and other departments

Table 9.4 Next steps of engagement after threat assessment

	Assessment of threat									
	Under		Appropriate		Over		Unsure		Total	
	N	(%)	N	(%)	N	(%)	N	(%)	N	(%)
Investigate (N=164)										
Yes	23	(79.3)	56	(91.8)	29	(93.5)	33	(76.7)	141	(86.0)
No	1	(3.4)	0	(0.0)	0	(0.0)	0	(0.0)	1	(0.6)
Don't know/No answer	5	(17.2)	5	(8.2)	2	(6.5)	10	(23.3)	22	(13.4)
TMT contacted (N=164)										
Yes	16	(55.2)	39	(63.9)	30	(96.8)	29	(67.4)	114	(69.5)
No	11	(37.9)	17	(27.9)	1	(3.2)	11	(25.6)	40	(24.4)
Don't know/No answer	2	(6.9)	5	(8.2)	0	(0.0)	3	(7.0)	10	(6.1)
Reasons for contacting TMT (N=167)										
TMT lead should be notified of potential threat/investigation steps	13	(39.4)	16	(25.4)	10	(45.5)	14	(28.6)	53	(31.7)
TMT lead can provide assistance/instruction	3	(9.1)	14	(22.2)	8	(36.4)	8	(16.3)	33	(19.8)
Company policy dictates it	0	(0.0)	1	(1.6)	0	(0.0)	1	(2.0)	2	(1.2)
No physical violence/threat of damage to property	3	(9.1)	2	(3.2)	0	(0.0)	1	(2.0)	6	(3.6)
Unknown extent of threats	11	(33.3)	19	(30.2)	2	(9.1)	20	(40.8)	52	(31.1)
Other	1	(3.0)	5	(7.9)	2	(9.1)	3	(6.1)	11	(6.6)
No answer	2	(6.1)	6	(9.5)	0	(0.0)	2	(4.1)	10	(6.0)

"unknown extent of threat," particularly among the under-assessors (33%) and those unsure of the threat level (41%).

Discussion

In the study, we found a variance in threat assessment levels whereby experienced team members were more likely to under-assess the level of threat. These team members' experiences may be the reason for their under-assessment; since they have responded to more cases, they may find any given level of threat to be less acute. Inaccurate assessment does not imply that the next steps in the investigation process would be impaired in any way. Indeed, the first assessment is a quick read on a case and will evolve as more information is collected. However, the most efficient response will arise from a team that has consistency in its ability to assess the threat level. Under-assessment could lead to reduced prioritization of next steps, while over-assessment could lead to over-investment in prioritizing a response, which would likely be costly to the business.

Company policies can provide one of the best sources for consistent assessment, but the majority of the team members participating in the study, even the more experienced ones, did not immediately identify the correct company policy at the beginning of this training. This implies that ongoing training to keep teams aware of company resources is necessary.

The initial assessment level was not strongly associated with subsequent actions, as further investigation was the overwhelming and correct next step. However, the level of assessed threat was associated with the likelihood of engaging the TMT as opposed to continuing investigation steps independently. Individuals who perceived a great threat were more likely to engage the team, while nearly half of those under-assessing the threat did not recommend engaging the team. The company policy encourages early engagement with the TMT so that information can be shared and investigative steps comprehensive. Even if all the next actions fall within one unit, the team should be informed and aware of these actions. Thus, under-assessment of the threat level may lead to a delay in team engagement.

This study provides evidence that assessing the level of threat can be a difficult and complex process with high individual variation. The study company has clear guidelines and ongoing training for its TMT members, and this training is likely an important component of a consistent response to threat management. It is unclear exactly how these findings within a company with progressive workplace violence policies and training might generalize to other companies, but it is reasonable to expect that variation in the threat assessment level would be even broader. Therefore, consistent approaches to threat level assessment and response are needed in business settings to reduce this variation, increase efficiency, and respond effectively.

References

ASIS/SHRM, *Workplace Violence Prevention and Intervention*, American National Standard (2011). Report No WVPI.1-2011.

Borum, R., Fein, R., Vossekuil, B., Berglund, J., Threat assessment: Defining an approach to assessing risk for targeted violence, *Behavioral Sciences and the Law*, 17, 323–337 (1999).

Bureau of Labor Statistics, Survey of Workplace Violence Prevention, 2005. U.S. Department of Labor (2006). Report No USDL 06-1860. Available at: www.bls.gov/iif/oshwc/osnr0026.pdf.

Bureau of Labor Statistics, National Census of Fatal Occupational Injuries in 2014 (Preliminary Results), U.S. Department of Labor (2015). Report No USDL-15-1789.

Calhoun, T., Weston, S., *Contemporary Threat Management*, San Diego, CA: Specialized Training Services (2003).

Callahan, M.R., Art imitates worklife: The world according to PACT, *Training and Development Journal*, 40, 56–59 (1986).

Chauhan, D.S., Preventing violence in the workplace: Threat assessment and prevention strategies, *Public Administration and Management: An Interactive Journal*, 4, 3, 370–383 (1999).

Clements, P.T., DeRanieri, J.T., Clark, K., Manno, M.S., Kuhn, D.W., Workplace violence and corporate policy for health care settings, *Nursing Economics*, 3, 23, 1–10 (2005).

Fein, R.A., Vossekuil, B., Holden, G.A., Threat assessment: An approach to prevent targeted violence, US Department of Justice, National Institute of Justice, Washington, DC (1995). Report No NCJ 155000. Available at: www.ncjrs.gov/pdffiles/threat.pdf.

FEMA, National Incident Management System (2015). Available at: www.fema.gov/national-incident-management-system.

Howard, J.L., Workplace violence in organizations: An exploratory study of organizational prevention techniques, *Employee Responsibilities and Rights Journal*, 13, 2, 57–75 (2001).

Kenny, J., Risk assessment and management teams: A comprehensive approach to early intervention in workplace violence, *Journal of Applied Security Research*, 5, 159–175 (2010).

McNiel, D.E., Chamberlain, J.R., Weaver, C.M., Hall, S.E., Fordwood, S.R., Binder, R.L., Impact of clinical training on violence risk assessment, *Education in Psychiatry*, 165, 2, 195–200 (2008).

Meloy, J.R., Hoffmann, J., Guldimann, A., James, D., The role of warning behaviors in threat assessment: An exploration and suggested typology, *Behavioral Sciences and the Law*, 30, 256–279 (2012).

Reynolds, K., Miles, H.L., The effect of training on the quality of HCR-20 violence risk assessments in forensic secure services, *The Journal of Forensic Psychiatry & Psychology*, 20, 3, 473–480 (2009).

Schat, A.C.H., Frone, M.R., Kelloway, E.K., Prevalence of workplace aggression in the U.S. workforce: Findings from a national study. In: Kelloway, E.K., Barling, J., Hurrell, J.J., eds., *Handbook of Workplace Violence*, Thousand Oaks, CA: Sage, 47–89 (2006).

Securitas, Top security threats and management issues facing corporate America, 2014, Parsippany, NJ: Securitas (2015).

Storey, J.E., Gibas, A.L., Reeves, K.A., Hart, S.D., Evaluation of a violence risk (threat) assessment training program for police and other criminal justice professionals, *Criminal Justice and Behavior*, 38, 6, 554–564 (2011).

Wade, J., Reducing the threat, *Risk Management Magazine*, 51, 10–18 (2004).

Bibliography

Alvarez, Gregory T., Ruff, Jason E., Private-sector employees and workplace privacy in the electronic era, *New Jersey Lawyer*, August, 24 (2007).

Arbuckle, J., Olson, L., Howard, M., Brillman, J., Ancti, C., Sklar, D. Safe at home? Domestic violence and other homicides among women in Mexico, *Annals of Emergency Medicine*, 27, 2, 210–215 (1996).

ASIS Commission on Standards and Guidelines, Workplace Violence Prevention and Intervention Standard (2011).

ASIS International, Workplace Violence Prevention and Response Guidelines (2005).

ASIS/SHRM, *Workplace Violence Prevention and Intervention*, American National Standard (2011).

Baum, Katrina, Catalano, Shannan, Rand, Michael, Rose, Kristina, *Stalking Victimization in the United States*, Washington, DC: Bureau of Justice Statistics (2009).

Beaver, Stephen J., Beyond the exclusivity rule: Employer's liability for workplace violence, 81 *Marquette Law Review* 103, 104–105 (1997).

Blythe, B., *Blindsided: A Manager's Guide to Catastrophic Incidents in the Workplace*, New York: Penguin (2002).

Borum, R., Fein, R., Vossekuil, B., Berglund, J., Threat assessment: Defining an approach to assessing risk for targeted violence, *Behavioral Sciences and the Law*, 17, 323–337 (1999).

Braverman, Mark, *Preventing Workplace Violence: A Guide for Employers and Practitioners*, California: Sage (1999).

Bureau of Labor Statistics, Survey of Workplace Violence Prevention, 2005, U.S. Department of Labor (2006). Report No USDL 06-1860. Available at: www.bls.gov/iif/oshwc/osnr0026.pdf

Bureau of Labor Statistics, National Census of Fatal Occupational Injuries in 2014 (Preliminary Results), U.S. Department of Labor (2015). Report No USDL-15-1789.

Calhoun, F.S., Weston, S.W., *Contemporary Threat Management: A Practical Guide for Identifying, Assessing and Managing Individuals of Violent Intent*, San Diego, CA: Specialized Training Services.

Callahan, M.R., Art imitates worklife: The world according to PACT, *Training and Development Journal*, 40, 56–59 (1986).

Campbell, J.C., Nursing assessment of risk of homicide for battered women, *Advances in Nursing Science*, 8, 4, 36–51 (1986).

Campbell, J.C., Prediction of homicide of and by battered women, in Campbell, J.C., ed., *Assessing the Risk of Dangerousness: Potential for Further Violence of Sexual Offenders, Batterers, and Child Abusers*, Newbury Park, CA: Sage, 96–113 (1995).

Campbell, Jacquelyn, Commentary on Websdale, lethality assessment approaches: reflections on their use and ways forward, *Violence against Women*, 11, 9, 1214–1221 (2005). Available at: www.baylor.edu/content/services/document.php/28821.pdf.

Campbell, J.C., Webster, D., Koziol-McLain, J., Block, C.R., Campbell, D.W., Curry, M.A., Gary, F.A., Glass, N.E., McFarlane, J., Sachs, C.J., Sharps, P.W., Ulrich, Y., Wilt, S.A., Assessing risk factors for intimate partner homicide, *National Institute of Justice Journal*, 250, 14–19 (2003).

CDC/NIOSH, Violence, *Occupational Hazards in Hospitals* (2002).

Chauhan, D.S. Preventing violence in the workplace: Threat assessment and prevention strategies, *Public Administration and Management: An Interactive Journal*, 4, 3, 370–383 (1999).

Clements, P.T., DeRanieri, J.T., Clark, K., Manno, M.S., Kuhn, D.W., Workplace violence and corporate policy for health care settings, *Nursing Economics*, 3, 23, 1–10 (2005).

Committee on Oversight and Government Reform, U.S. House of Representatives, Staff Report, *Slipping through the Cracks: How the D.C. Navy Yard Shooting Exposes Flaws in the Federal Security Clearance Process*, Washington, DC (2014).

Corcoran, Michael H., Cawood, James S., *Violence Assessment and Intervention, The Practitioner's Handbook*, New York: CRC Press (2003).

Daly, M., Wiseman, K.A., Wilson, M., Women with children sired by previous partners incur excess risk of uxoricide, *Homicide Studies*, 1, 1, 61–71 (1997).

Dansie, Susan J., *Lethality Assessment and Safety Planning* (1992). Available at: www.ncdsv.org/images/Let halityAssessmentSafetyPlanning.pdf.

De Becker, G., and Associates, Domestic Violence Method (DV MOSAIC) (2000). Available at: www.mosaicmethod.com.

Deisinger, Gene, Randazzo, Marisa, O'Neill, Daniel, Savage, Jenna, *The Handbook for Campus Threat Assessment and Management Teams*, Massachusetts: Applied Risk Management (2008).

Elliott, J.F. (ed.), *Workplace Violence Prevention: A Practical Guide* (2 vols), Vancouver, BC: Specialty Technical Publishers (2003).

Fein, Robert, Vossekuil, Bryan, Holden, G.A., *Threat Assessment: An Approach to Prevent Targeted Violence*, Washington, DC: U.S. Department of Justice, Office of Justice Programs (1995). Available at: www.ncjrs.gov/pdffiles/threat.pdf.

Fein, Robert, Vossekuil, Bryan, Pollack, William S., Borum, Randy, Modzeleski, William, Reddy, Marisa, *Threat Assessment in Schools: A Guide to Managing Threatening Situations and Creating Safe School Climates*, Washington, DC: U.S. Secret Service and U.S. Department of Education (2002).

FEMA. National Incident Management System (2015). Available at: www.fema.gov/national-incident-management-system.

Gelles, R., Lethality and Risk Assessment for Family Violence Cases, paper presented at the 4th International Conference on Children Exposed to Family Violence, San Diego, CA, October 1998.

Goodman, L., Dutton, M.A., Bennett, L., Predicting repeat abuse among arrested batterers: Use of the Danger Assessment Scale in the criminal justice system, *Journal of Interpersonal Violence*, 10, 63–74 (2000).

Hare, R.D., *Without Conscience: The Disturbing World of the Psychopaths Among Us*, New York: Pocket Books (1993).

Heckert, D.A., Gondolf, E.W., Battered women's perceptions of risk versus risk factors and instruments in predicting repeat reassault, *Journal of Interpersonal Violence*, 19, 7, 778–800 (2004).

Howard, J.L., Workplace violence in organizations: An exploratory study of organizational prevention techniques, *Employee Responsibilities and Rights Journal*, 13, 2, 57–75 (2001).

Injury Prevention Research Center, University of Iowa, *Workplace Violence—A Report to the Nation* (2001).

Kenny, J. Risk assessment and management teams: A comprehensive approach to early intervention in workplace violence, *Journal of Applied Security Research*, 5, 159–175 (2010).

Kiesel, Diane, Domestic Violence: Law Policy and Practice, Newark, NJ: LexisNexis Matthew Bender (2007), published by Safe Horizon, available at: www.safehorizon.org/page/domestic-violence-statistics-facts-52.html.

Lansu, Michael, Nadia Ezaldein fatally shot in shooting at downtown Nordstrom, Chicago: The Chicago Sun-times (2014). Available at: http://homicides.suntimes.com/2014/11/30/nadia-ezaldein-fatally-shot-in-shooting-at-downtown-nordstrom/.

Lemon, Nancy K.D., Domestic Violence Law, St. Paul, MN: LEG, Inc. doing business as West Academic (2013).

Lies, Mark A. II, *Preventing and Managing Workplace Violence, Legal and Strategic Guidelines*, Chicago, IL: ABA (2008).

Littler Mendelson, *The National Employer*.

McNiel, D.E., Chamberlain, J.R., Weaver, C.M., Hall, S.E., Fordwood, S.R., Binder, R.L., Impact of clinical training on violence risk assessment, *Education in Psychiatry*, 165, 2, 195–200 (2008).

Mahoney, Martha, *Legal Images of Battered Women: Redefining the Issue of Separation*, Ann Arbor, MI: The Michigan Law Review Association (1991).

Meloy, J. Reid, *The Psychology of Stalking, Clinical and Forensic Perspectives*, San Diego, CA: Academic (1998).

Meloy, J. Reid, *Violence Risk and Threat Assessment*, San Diego, CA: Specialized Training Services (2000).

Meloy, J. Reid, Hoffmann, J., Guldimann, A., James, D., The role of warning behaviors in threat assessment: An exploration and suggested typology, *Behavioral Sciences and the Law*, 30, 256–279 (2012).

Meloy, J. Reid, O'Toole, Mary Ellen, The concept of leakage in threat assessment, *Behavioral Science and the Law*, 513–527 (2011).

National Center for Victims of Crime, Stalking Resource Center, *Fact Sheet on Stalking*. Available at: http://victimsofcrime.org/docs/default-source/src/stalking-fact-sheet-2015_eng.pdf?sfvrsn=2.

NIOSH, *Violence in the Workplace, Risk Factors and Prevention Strategies*, Washington, DC (1996).

OSHA, National Institute for Occupational Safety and Health (NIOSH), *Enforcement Procedures for Investigating or Inspecting Workplace Violence Incidents*, Washington, DC (September, 2011).

O'Toole, Mary Ellen, *The School Shooter: A Threat Assessment Perspective*, Quantico, VA: Critical Incident Response Group, National Center for the Analysis of Violent Crime, FBI Academy (1999).

Paziotopoulos, Pam, Domestic violence and the workplace, *Workplace Violence Prevention Book*, C TAB F, Specialty Technical Publishers Reference Guide, STP Publishers, chapter 1 (2002).

Paziotopoulos, P., Domestic violence in the workplace, in Elliott, J.F., ed., *Workplace Violence Prevention: A Practical Guide*, Vancouver, BC: Specialty Technical Publishers, 1–39 (2002).

Paziotopoulos, Pam, Runge, Robin, What employers can do to minimize the impact of domestic violence and stalking in the workplace, in *Preventing and Managing Workplace Violence: Legal and Strategic Guidelines*, Lies, Mark A., ed., Chicago, IL: ABA, 258–290 (2008).

Peek-Asa, Corinne, Casteel, Carri, Rugala, Eugene A., Romano, S., Ramirez, M., Workplace violence investigations and activation of the threat management teams in a multinational corporation, *Journal of Occupational and Environmental Medicine*, 55, 1305–1311 (2013).

Peek-Asa, Corinne, Casteel, Carri, Rugala, Eugene A., Holbrook, Christina, Bixler, David, Ramirez, Marizen, The threat management assessment and response model: A conceptual plan for threat management and training, *Security Journal Magazine*, 30, 3, 940–950 (2015).

Prevention of Workplace Violence in Healthcare and Social Assistance, Occupational Safety and Health Administration, January 7, 2016, F.R. Doc No. 2016–29197, available at: www.osha.gov/pls/oshaweb/owadisp.show_document?p_table=FEDERAL_REGISTER&p_id=27581.

Reynolds, K., Miles, H.L., The effect of training on the quality of HCR-20 violence risk assessments in forensic secure services, *The Journal of Forensic Psychiatry & Psychology*, 20, 3, 473–480 (2009).

Riley, Kyle, Employer TROS are all the rage: A new approach to workplace violence, 4 *Nevada Law Journal*, 1, 4 (2003).

Roehl, Janice, O'Sullivan, Chris, Webster, Daniel, Campbell, Jacquelyn, *Intimate Partner Violence Risk Assessment Validation Study, Final Report*, published by Safe Horizon (2005), available at: www.safehorizon.org/page/domestic-violence-statistics-facts-52.html.

Romano, S.J., *Communication Survival Skills for Managers*, FBI Law Enforcement Bulletin (2002).

Romano, S.J., Rugala, E.A. et al., *Workplace Violence: Prevention, Readiness and Response*, FBI Law Enforcement Bulletin (January 2011).

Rugala, E.A., *Workplace Violence: Issues in Response*, Quantico, VA: Critical Incident Response Group, National Center for the Analysis of Violence Crime, FBI Academy (2004).

Rugala, E.A., Fitzgerald, J.R., Workplace violence: From threat to intervention, *Clinics in Occupational and Environmental Medicine*, 3, 775–789 (2003).

Rugala, E.A., Isaacs, A., *Workplace Violence: Issues in Response*, Critical Incident Response Group, National Center for the Analysis of Violent Crime, FBI Academy, Quantico, VA (2004).

Rugala, E.A., McNamara, J., Wattendorf, G., *Expert Testimony and Risk Assessment in Stalking Cases: The FBI's National Center for the Analysis of Violent Crime*, FBI Law Enforcement Bulletin 73, 11 (2004).

Sampson, Richard T., Topazian, Johnathan R., Violence in the workplace, *For the Defense* (December 1996).

Schat, A.C.H., Frone, M.R., Kelloway, E.K., Prevalence of workplace aggression in the U.S. workforce: Findings from a national study, in Kelloway, E.K., Barling, J., Hurrell, J.J., eds., *Handbook of Workplace Violence*, Thousand Oaks, CA: Sage 47–89 (2006).

Sciara, Susan, Employee assistance programs, in Elliott, J.F. (ed.), *Workplace Violence Prevention: A Practical Guide* (2 vols), Vancouver, BC: Specialty Technical Publishers (2003).

Securitas, Top Security Threats and Management Issues facing Corporate America, 2014, Parsippany, NJ: Securitas (2015).

Speer, R., and contributors, *Workplace Violence Prevention and Intervention*, American National Standard, Alexandria, Virginia (2011), available at: www.asisonline.org.

Speer, Rebecca, Workplace violence: A legal perspective, *Clinics in Occupational and Environmental Medicine*, 3, 733–749 (2003).

Stalking Resource Center website: http://victimsofcrime.org/our-programs/stalking-resource-center.

Storey, J.E., Gibas, A.L., Reeves, K.A., Hart, S.D., Evaluation of a violence risk (threat) assessment training program for police and other criminal justice professionals, *Criminal Justice and Behavior*, 38, 6, 554–564 (2011).

United States Bureau of Labor Statistics (2015).

United States Department of Labor, *DOL Workplace Violence Program – Appendices* (last visited February 22, 2017), available at: www.dol.gov/oasam/hrc/policies/dol-workplace-violence-program-appendices.htm.

United States Department of Labor, State Plan Adoption of OSHA's Revised Reporting Requirements (29 CFR 1904.39), available at: www.osha.gov/recordkeeping2014/state_adoption_table.html.

University of Iowa, Injury Prevention Research Center, *Workplace Violence—A Report to the Nation* (2001).

Van Hasselt, V.B., Flood, J.J., Romano, S.J., Vecchi, G.M., de Fabrique, N., Dalfonzo, V.A., Hostage-taking in the context of domestic violence: Some case examples, *Journal of Family Violence*, 20, 21–26 (2005).

Wade, J., Reducing the threat, *Risk Management Magazine*, 51, 10–18 (2004).

Wagage, Suraji R., When the consequences are life and death: Pretrial detention for domestic violence offenders, 7 *Drexel Law Review*, 195, 211 (2014).

Weisz, A., Tolman, R., Saunders, D.G., Assessing the risk of severe domestic violence, *Journal of Interpersonal Violence*, 15, 1, 75–90 (2000).

White, Jennifer Heidt, Text message monitoring after Quon v. Arch Wireless: What private employers need to know about the Stored Communications Act and an employee's right to privacy, 5 *Shidler Journal of Law, Commerce & Technology*, 19, 12 (2009).

Wilkinson, Carol, Peek-Asa, Corinne, Violence in the workplace, *Clinics in Occupational and Environmental Medicine*, 3, 775–789 (2003).

Williams, K.R., Houghton, A.B., Assessing the risk of domestic violence re-offending: A validation study, *Law and Human Behavior*, 28, 437–455 (2004).

www.cindysmemorial.org.

www.cnn.com/2013/12/06/us/domestic-intimate-partner-violence-fast-facts/index.html.

www.dir.ca.gov/dosh/dosh_publications/IIPP.html#30.

www.law.cornell.edu/constitution/fourth_amendment.

www.parking.org/wp-content/uploads/2016/01/TPP-2014-03-Guns-In-the-Lot.pdf.

Index

Note: Page numbers in **bold** refer to tables and in *italics* refer to figures.

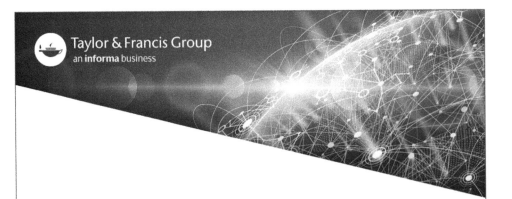

For Product Safety Concerns and Information please contact our EU
representative GPSR@taylorandfrancis.com
Taylor & Francis Verlag GmbH, Kaufingerstraße 24, 80331 München, Germany

www.ingramcontent.com/pod-product-compliance
Ingram Content Group UK Ltd.
Pitfield, Milton Keynes, MK11 3LW, UK
UKHW051833180425
457613UK00022B/1235